Reading Projects
Reimagined

Student-Driven Conferences
to Deepen Critical Thinking

DAN FEIGELSON

HEINEMANN
Portsmouth, NH

Heinemann

361 Hanover Street

Portsmouth, NH 03801–3912

www.heinemann.com

Offices and agents throughout the world

Library of Congress Cataloging-in-Publication Data

Feigelson, Daniel H.

   Reading projects reimagined : student-driven conferences to deepen critical thinking / Daniel Feigelson.

      pages cm

   ISBN 978-0-325-05127-7

   1. Reading (Elementary).   I. Title.

   LB1573.F36 2014

   372.4—dc23   2014018179

Editor: Holly Kim Price

Production: Hilary Goff

Cover and interior designs: Suzanne Heiser

Photo credits: Mary Cybulski, Lisa A. Fowler, Michael Grover

Typesetter: Publishers' Design and Production Services, Inc.

Manufacturing: Steve Bernier

Printed in the United States of America on acid-free paper

18 17 16 15 14 VP 1 2 3 4 5

For Sonia and Kiri

Two deep thinkers

Two very different readers

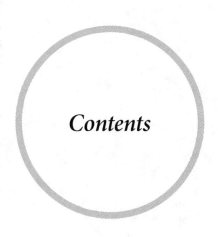

Contents

Acknowledgments

I once heard it said of Shelley Harwayne that the interesting thing about talking with her is when she leaves, you continue the conversation in your head.

It was that way with this book. Some significant conversations with a few brilliant people sparked my thinking. As I talked back to these folks in my head, ideas began to take shape.

My literary partnership with John Tintori began at a dinner party. After several drinks, the discussion somehow turned to *The Brothers Karamazov* by Dostoyevsky. "That book is around a thousand pages long, and every character has something like three different names," I said to no one in particular. "It's the kind of book someone would have to force you to read." John looked up defiantly from behind his glass of bourbon and said, "I'm going to force you to read it." "Oh yeah?" I responded. "I'm going to force *you* to read it." More than twenty years later, we are still at it. I read with John in mind, anticipating what he may or may not find interesting. It occurred to me that if students in classrooms could get to know themselves and their classmates in a similar way, they might read more deeply.

At an outdoor café in Orlando, Florida, Kate Montgomery sparked another internal conversation. Kate was the editor of my first book for Heinemann, and we were at the NCTE conference brainstorming new topics. "So what have you been working on with teachers in classrooms these days?" she asked. I began speaking excitedly about the reading conferences I'd been having lately and how much more engaged the kids seemed when they did work based on their own ideas. "Hmm," Kate mused. "You know, it's been a while since anyone has thought about reading projects. Maybe you can be the one to look at them differently." At first I was skeptical; the term "reading projects" conjured unpleasant images. In the weeks that followed though, I began to wonder—wasn't a project, by definition, something you care and think deeply about? Did a reading project have to take a long time, or was it possible to come up with "quick and dirty" work that could help students understand more deeply without taking too much time away from reading? Could project work come from a student's thinking, rather than a teacher's agenda? Kate's casual suggestion raised some big questions, which are explored in these pages.

In the beginning stages of writing this book, I went out to breakfast with long-time compadre Ralph Fletcher and shared some of my initial ideas. At that time, the working title was *Making Comprehension Concrete*. Ralph was dubious. "Let me get this straight," he said. "When students do this work, the teacher gets a window into their thinking. So that helps with assessment, right?" "Correct," I responded. Ralph shook his head. "Not a good enough reason," he answered. "I get why it's good for the teacher, but what's in it for the kid?" Following this conversation, I became much more focused on helping children name their *own* ideas—making them co-conspirators in their own comprehension.

Perhaps the single conversation that inspired me most was the one I had with my daughter Sonia when she was nine years old, recounted in this book's Introduction. As an even younger child, she liked to remind me, "You may tell me what to do, but I am the boss of my own brain!" This admonishment, and Sonia's strong sense of individuality, is what made me want to champion the cause of "thinking about what *I* want to think about," for all children.

The work of several friends, colleagues, and thought partners has been just as influential. Ellin Keene, fellow comprehension activist, has taught me more about reading than any other individual. My good buddy and fellow Beatles fanatic Carl Anderson has paved the way for all of us when it comes to thinking about conferring. Old friend Kathy Collins and newer colleague Matt Glover confer with little guys in a similar way to what I do with older students. Lucy Calkins' reminder that "Every child has a story to tell; the question is whether they tell it to *you*," has guided my thinking not only in this book but throughout my career. Lastly, any work involving the way teachers speak to students owes a lot to Peter Johnston. I'm not sure whether to thank or curse him for the way he has made me second-guess the language I use with children.

There are many teachers, literacy coaches, and principals who have contributed to the thinking in these pages. First and foremost, I've had the exquisite good fortune to be part of a reading think tank at Manhattan New School (aka PS 290), where many of these ideas were conceived and piloted. It began with me leading the professional development but evolved into an equal partnership; Jamie Kushner, Joanne Searle, Sophie Brady, Ali Gold, Leslie Profeta, Hallie Saltz, and especially Principal Sharon Hill at MNS are truly the book's co-authors. The teachers of PS 33 in Chelsea have also made big contributions, figuring out innovative strategies for moving the work from grade to grade; Alycia Zimmerman, Aly Miller, Susan Myung, Tom Kelly, Yanik Breving, and Principal Linore Lindy, in particular, have been brilliant collaborators. Kara Pranikoff and Namrata Kakkar's work on talk and comprehension at PS 234 has influenced my thinking significantly as well. Elsewhere in New York City, Nancy Wahl and Principal Kelly Shannon of PS 41; Clarissa Isaac and Principal Melissa Rodriguez of PS 137; Lauren Brown and Principal Lisa Ripperger of PS 234; Yolen Medard, Kay Loua, and Principals Dean Ketchum and Ryan Bourke of Midtown

West; Shannon Potts, Noah Gordon, and Principal Katie Banucci-Smith of Special Music School; Nikki Blaise, Zehra Haider, Chris Ruggi, Diane Yamada, Laura Salman, and Principal Irene Sanchez of PS 15; Eileen Delucia and Principals Racquel Jones and Sameer Talati of PS/IS 7; Principal Rhonda Levy and her heroic staff at PS 142; the intrepid teachers of River East School and their Principals Alison McKenzie and Rob Catlin, have all added their keen insights. Barbara Lindsay, Christine Leahy, Leanne Grant, Bonnie Marsette, and the entire Westwood, Massachusetts, school district deserve much credit for their fearless explorations. Thanks as well to some folks out in Jersey—a tip of the hat to Christine Landwehrle of Rumson, Mercedes Berrios of Upper Deerfield, and my old pal Jodi Mahoney over in South Brunswick. Lara Burenin, David Konigsberg, Kara Pranikoff, and Gabriel Feldberg all read early drafts and gave valuable feedback.

Looking to the future, I am honored and jazzed to be co-conspiring with Shelley Harwayne (again!), Sharon Taberski, Grant Wiggins, Mary Anne Sacco, Deborah Kenny, Zoltan Sarda, Donna Santman, Barry Hoonan, Bill Fulbrecht, Ellen Rice, Melanie Bryon, and my other brilliant new colleagues at Harlem Village Academies. More comprehension conversations are sure to be forthcoming in such illustrious company.

Holly Kim Price at Heinemann is quite simply the best editor in the world and maybe the first person ever to succeed in keeping me (well, sort of) to a deadline. Thanks to Lisa Fowler for coming all the way to New York City to take pictures of some of the kids and teachers who brought this work to life. Hilary Goff's graphic vision has made this book more than just words on paper. Finally, my dear friend and photographer par excellence, Mary Cybulski (here's to the women's auxiliary!) saved the day with her Canon camera.

On another note, thanks to Jerry, Mehgan, and Clare of Rev Cafe in Hudson, New York, for providing me with coffee, a place to work, and just enough (but not too many) distractions. At least half the book was written at this fabulous establishment.

Just before the finish line, I experienced a brush with mortality that put many things in perspective. Thanks to Dr. Richard Stein, Dr. Leonard Girardi, and my cousin/alter ego Dr. Elizabeth Feigelson for saving my life.

My daughter Kiri Hogue has a singular talent for getting to the heart of the matter and an uncanny radar for feelings and relationships. Her sensitivity to what is going on in people's heads helped inspire the idea that teachers must look below the surface to really understand children, as readers and as human beings.

My love, Cara, has been more than patient as I've hidden away for hours and days to write. She has read draft after draft, listened as I've gone on and on about small details, and generally put up with my obsessive behavior. More important, she has been playful when I was irrational, taken the long view when I was lost in minutiae, and provided love when I was most discouraged. There is no way this book would have happened without her.

Here's to freedom of thought.

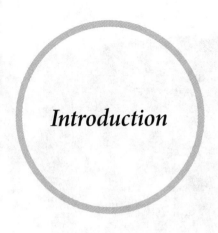

Introduction

What I Want to Think About

> *Sapere aude!*
> *(Have the courage to make use of your own understanding!)*
> —*Immanuel Kant, 1784, after Homer*

My daughter Sonia has always been an avid reader. In her early years, we often discussed books—at breakfast, on the playground, at bedtime—and she was never at a loss for an opinion. So I was a bit taken aback when Sonia came home one day from fourth grade and angrily announced, "Dad, I *hate* reading response."

"Really?" I asked. "That surprises me. You love to talk about books."

"Well, yes," she answered in an exasperated tone. "But listen to *this*." Sonia fished out a sheet of paper from her backpack, and read in her best boring grown-up voice: "*Why do you think the fairy hid the key? What would you do if you were Jane? What is the author trying to tell us about friendship?*"

At this, she stuffed the paper back in its folder. "Well, Ms. Simms," she snapped angrily, "that is a great reading response. But it's *YOUR* reading response. It's not what *I* want to think about."

The truth is, most children spend an awful lot of time in school answering comprehension questions posed by teachers. Some of these questions may be at a basic retell level, repeating back "what happened." Some may be more sophisticated, designed to push the reader's thinking further. Both have their place and purpose. Part of a reading teacher's job is to assess students' understanding, and part of it is to provide them with new ways to look at texts—introduce literary elements, teach them to be proficient readers of nonfiction. But Sonia's fourth-grade complaint raises important questions: *Should there also be a place in the day where we teach students to come up with their **own** ideas, without teacher prompting? And how do we do this while still maintaining a sense of rigor and accountability?*

Literacy standards such as the Common Core stress that readers should understand what the author is saying and also be able to create and defend their own arguments using text-based evidence (National Governors Association 2010). Typically, teachers address this by asking clever questions designed to move children to think more deeply. But what happens when students leave school and encounter complex texts without anyone there to tell them what to think about? While thoughtful teacher questions can nudge young readers to think about books in new ways, it doesn't necessarily follow that they will then be able to come up with a line of thinking on their own. As Richard Allington flatly states, "Students do not develop comprehension strategies by answering questions after reading" (2006).

To be clear, Allington's words of caution do *not* mean that we should never ask children questions about their books. As Ellin Keene reminds us, "Comprehension questions can be valuable assessment, but don't kid yourself you are *teaching* them something" (2007). Our job as teachers of reading is first and foremost to teach (and assess!) comprehension strategies, but we also need to help students learn to use these strategies *independently*.

The Content of Comprehension

Carl Anderson (2001) points out the irony of the fact that science, social studies, and math are referred to as the "content" areas. This seems to suggest that reading and writing are somehow *non*-content subjects, disciplines where we somehow magically intuit what to do. Nothing could be further from the truth. Teachers of reading know very well that there are specific things a student needs to know and be able to do in order to understand. It can be helpful to think of this *content of comprehension* as falling into two basic categories: **text-based** and **metacognitive**.

On the ***text-based*** side, students need to learn *how* particular genres of text are put together. Certainly a reader can understand a narrative more deeply when she or he is familiar with story elements. *Where is the conflict? How do the setting and character descriptions help us understand the story? Exactly what themes does the author want us to come away thinking about?* Similarly, knowing something about informational text features helps a reader keep track of the many facts typically included in an article or a textbook. Indeed, there's a considerable amount to know about all this external "stuff"—how the text is structured—that's quite apart from what we do in our heads to make meaning.

Equally critical is ***metacognitive***, or *strategy*, instruction. Important thinkers such as Ellin Keene (2008, 2012), Stephanie Harvey (2000), and Richard Allington (2001), have pushed teachers to also devote instructional time to the internal process of reading, i.e., what we do in our heads to understand (Keene 2008). After the landmark book *Mosaic of Thought* came out in 1997, teachers around the country began to craft entire units of study on inference, synthesis, and monitoring for meaning. Phrases like *text-to-self*, *text-to-text*, and *text-to world* became common currency among students and teachers alike. As Keene and Zimmermann (2007) succinctly point out, "Skilled readers think about their thinking."

The truth is that as we actually read, these two things are not so divided. When readers decide for themselves what the important parts are, for example, they are picking up cues *in the text* about where to pay special attention. At the same time, our individual interests, prior knowledge, and purpose for reading—all in the reader's head—also influence how we determine importance. Nonetheless, from a teacher's point of view, it is helpful to think of these two instructional objectives as distinct. For one thing, as the standards emphasize, it is critical to be accountable to the text—*and* to differentiate our own opinion from what is actually there on the page. But it is also true that if the larger goal of learning to read is learning to think, we want students to know *how* to come up with their own ideas and keep track of them.

Most reading instruction is heavily weighted toward explicit instruction of these two types of content, and rightly so. Students are not likely to figure out on their own how to negotiate a complicated informational text, or realize that one way to think about narrative is in terms of problem and solution. Indeed, a teacher is not doing her job if she doesn't teach these skills and strategies. But at some point,

like it or not, readers will be faced with a complicated text and not have a teacher there to tell them what to think about. If our objective is for students to become independent thinkers (and comprehenders!), then some time must also be devoted to explicitly teaching students to use this content of comprehension on their own. And that means teaching them to recognize, name, and extend their *own* ideas about what they read.

The leap from coming up with a thoughtful answer to a teacher question, to independently asking and answering our *own* questions is not automatic. Knowing the content of comprehension is, of course, a critical first step. However, teaching children to use this knowledge to come up with and extend their own ideas looks different than content instruction.

Researchers like Nell Duke (2012) observe that the more *authentic* the reading experience, the more likely students are to retain what they learn. So what sorts of authentic experiences help students learn to develop their own ideas, without the teacher taking over? And what work can we assign in reading class so students continue to delve deeper into their own thinking when the grownup has gone away?

It is here that conference-based reading projects come in. The work assigned through these individual conversations is, first and foremost, a collaborative effort between teacher and student. It is a direct outgrowth of what the student says or does. The teacher's role is to listen carefully, help the reader name what she or he is beginning to think about, and—together—come up with an assignment that will extend that thinking. In the course of this targeted work, connections are made to future reading. The expectation is that the comprehension strategy will be applied to the next book, and the book after that.

This book is a guide to implementing these sorts of individual projects in an elementary or middle school reading classroom. It contains step-by-step guidelines outlining how to conduct a conference; categories to help teachers narrow down possible directions a conference could go; and examples of student work and teacher-student dialogue, to give a concrete picture of what it all looks and sounds like. To illustrate how such individual reading work fits into the larger context of a reading program, I begin with the diary account of a fourth-grade teacher, chronicling her work with one student over several months.

The book is for teachers, instructional coaches, school administrators, school districts, and any other educators interested in deepening the work in their reading classrooms. It is not intended to replace the work of an existing reading curriculum, nor does it suggest that teaching end-year expectations is less important than targeted, individual work. My hope is that it will inspire educators to think carefully about the balance between whole-class work designed to meet grade-specific standards, and individual assignments that teach students how to think for themselves. I'm not voting on what percentage of time should be spent on one versus the other; I'm suggesting that there should be at least *some* of each.

Katerina

SIX MONTHS IN THE LIFE OF A FOURTH-GRADE READER

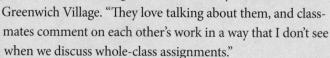

Katerina's Fourth-Grade Reading Projects, September to February

Independent reading projects that spring from children's thinking create a sense of ownership in the classroom, and a palpable buzz of excitement. "My students are always reminding me when it's time to share their projects," comments fifth-grade teacher Nancy Wahl, at PS 41 in Greenwich Village. "They love talking about them, and classmates comment on each other's work in a way that I don't see when we discuss whole-class assignments."

The sad truth, though, is that we only have so much time in a day, and lots of material to cover. Where does individual, conference-based work fit into a year-long curriculum? As valuable as these projects are, work that does not take the long view will have limited impact. If conferences do not connect from one to the next, it is unlikely children will retain what they have learned, let alone apply it to the next book.

What follows is a case study/diary from master teacher Jamie Kushner's fourth-grade inclusion classroom at Manhattan New School. It documents the work of Katerina, a grade level reader, for the first half of a school year. The notes, from Jamie's anecdotal records, illustrate one teacher's observations and reflections about one student. They give a clear sense of how independent, conference-based reading work can build across a school year—and how it fits with (or sometimes stands apart from) the rest of the curriculum.

September

What's happening in the classroom: We conducted beginning-year assessments, getting students into "just right books." I started out using our summer reading book, *Tales of a Fourth Grade Nothing*, to teach summarizing. Toward the end of September, we started discussing different types of thinking that readers can have about their books and worked on keeping track of our thoughts in Reading Notebooks.

Katerina's work: Katerina is reading *The BFG* by Roald Dahl and using sticky notes to record her thinking. At this early point in the year, she is coming up with lots of questions and looking for missing information—"Could it be someone from the orphanage?" "How do you collect a dream?" or guessing what will happen next, with occasional editorial comments—"I think they are becoming friends," "This seems a little dangerous!" (see Figure 1.1).

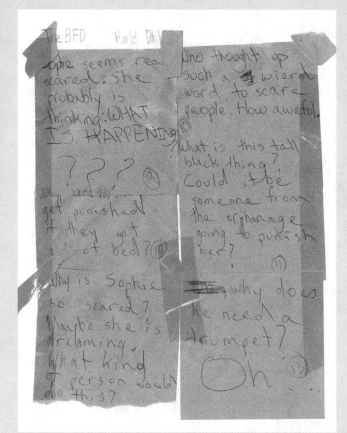

Figure 1.1 Katerina's early sticky notes, largely questions about what will happen next.

October

What's happening in the classroom: We started conferring and giving out individual reading projects. Since we didn't want students to feel that sticky notes were the only way to track their thinking—depending on their idea, a chart, list, or some other method might work better— we modeled different types of note-taking in our own Reading Notebooks. To build excitement and show how much we valued their independent work, we made time for students to share their reading projects with the rest of the class. Sometimes it would be finished work, but sometimes they'd just share how the conference went and the assignment they were about to start.

Katerina's work: At the beginning of the month, Katerina went a little further with her questioning, jotting wonderings in her notebook rather than on sticky notes, but also trying to answer her own questions, based on a whole-class lesson (see Figure 1.2).

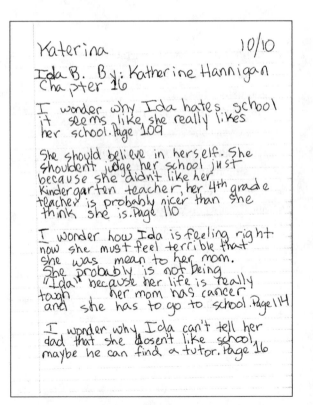

Figure 1.2 Katerina's October wonderings, with early attempts at answering her own questions

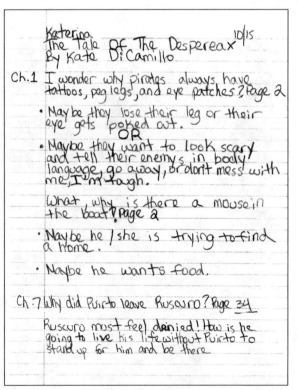

Figure 1.3 Katerina's October "or maybe" wonderings

A couple weeks in, Katerina moved to saying "or maybe" when answering her questions. This showed she was beginning to think of multiple possibilities, not just sticking with her first idea (see Figure 1.3).

First Project, October 16: Katerina was given her first conference-based individual project with *The Tale of Despereaux*. She identified a character trait ("Despereaux was brave"), and when I asked her to say more about that, she answered, "because he jumped through mouse traps, he doesn't cower, he reads books, he talks to the princess, and that's all breaking the rules of Mouse Town." Knowing that Katerina had begun to entertain multiple possibilities in thinking about her books, I asked if she thought *brave* was the *only* word to describe him. She thought not. I said, "In the books you are currently reading, characters are multi-dimensional, just like real people. We don't have one character trait, we have many, and so do these characters." We agreed that it would be interesting to look for evidence of at least two more traits and then write a reflection in her notebook about what she noticed (see Figures 1.4a–d).

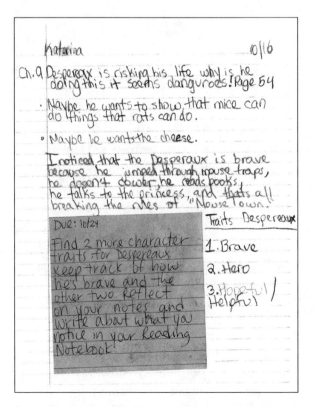
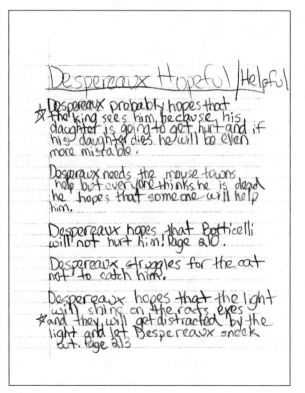

Figures 1.4a and 1.4b Katerina's *Despereaux* assignment

(continues)

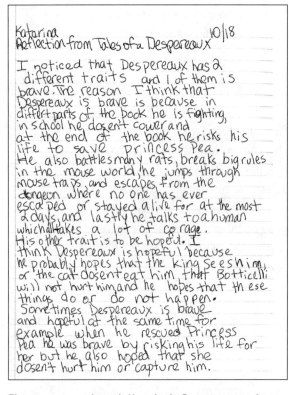

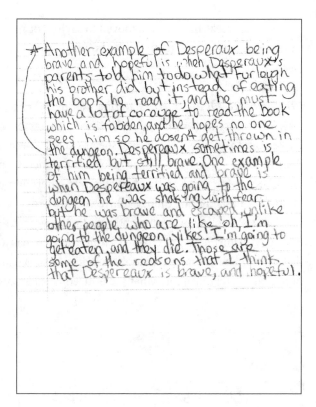

Figures 1.4c and 1.4d Katerina's *Despereaux* assignment

I was impressed at how quickly Katerina came up with more character traits and multiple examples to support her ideas. In my next conference, I decided to follow up with thinking about character but in another way, perhaps around character relationships.

Interestingly, a week later Katerina tried this same project in her next book, *A Wrinkle in Time* (see Figure 1.5); she noticed that one of the characters (Charles) was fearless and brave, and independently decided to track evidence for those two traits. We leveraged the opportunity and had her share her work with the rest of the class, saying, "How cool is this? Katerina is carrying her project over to the next book!"

November

What's happening in the classroom: We continued to model different ways to name an idea based on your own thoughts, and also how to track it in your notebook. Around the middle of the month, we challenged students to do this even when we had *not* given them a project. Students began taking notes as they read, with the aim of identifying an idea worth following.

HW
Katerina 10/23
A Wrinkle In Time
I noticed that Charles is fearless, and brave.
Im tracking places that show that Charles is fearless, and brave.
Charles was waiting at the bottom of their house in the midle of a hurricane.
Charles goes into a haunted house and meets Mrs. Whatsit, Mrs. Who, and Mrs. Which.
Charles was sitting at the dinner table and Mrs. Whatsit came into their house out of no where, and Charles ofers her a sandwitch.
Charles goes back to the haunted house and encorages Meg to go with him.
Charles asks Calvin to read to him
Charles wants to go save his dad!

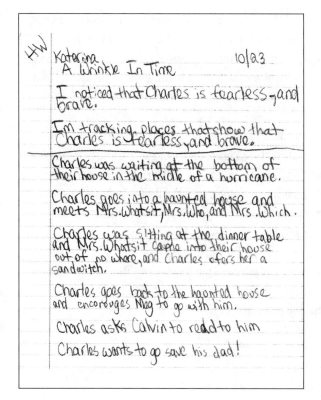

Figure 1.5 Katerina's *A Wrinkle in Time* work, independently carrying her project on to the next book

Katerina 11/5
Ella Enchanted by: Gail Carson Levine
Pg. 3 Ella is determand to break the curse that she will be obedient.
Pg. 3 I feel really bad for Ella's mom because E's mom is probably scared that if someone says "Cut you arm off." Ella will have to do it.
Pg. 3 I wonder why Lucinda will not undo the curse?
• Maybe she is evil
• Maybe she dosen't know how.
Pg. 5 Why cant Ella say NO to a comand?
Pg. 7 E's mom seems to take advantage of her curse.
Pg. 11 I wonder what is going to happen to Ella now that her mother died.
Pg. 16 Why didn't Prince Char take Ella.
Pg. 19 Ella seems to be very sad.
Pg. 30 Why didn't Mandy tell Ella earlyer she was her fairy god mother.

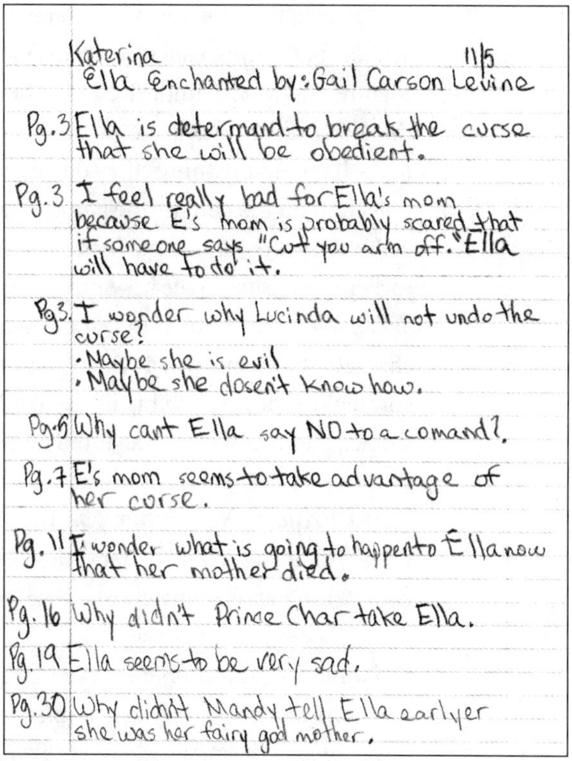

Figure 1.6 Katerina's *Ella Enchanted* work, searching for an idea to track

Katerina's work: Katerina started reading *Ella Enchanted* and took notes with the hope of finding an idea to track. She noticed that the character Mandy really cared about Ella, and was about to track this idea when we met for our next conference (see Figure 1.6).

Second Project, November 8: When I asked Katerina what she was thinking about, she spoke of Mandy and Ella. I could have assigned a project based on character relationships—and almost did—but we had talked about that in whole-class lessons and during read-aloud, so I worried that such a project wouldn't really push her thinking. I decided to try something more sophisticated. We started talking about the roles characters play in a text. "Authors are always making decisions when they write books. They not only choose every word carefully but also think deeply when deciding what characters to include. Have you ever thought about why an author chose to include a character in a book?"

Katerina thought it was an interesting idea. "Well," she reflected, "there are a lot of little characters—but I think Gail Carson Levine especially wants us to think about three of them: Ella, Mandy, and Mom." Impressed with how quickly she narrowed it down, I challenged Katerina to think about the roles those characters play. "Why does the author include those characters and make them do the things they do? Remember to include evidence from the text. Then write a reflection on the choices the author makes."

I wasn't sure if I had made the correct decision and decided to check Katerina's notebook earlier than usual to see how the project was going (see Figures 1.7a and 1.7b). She had written, "Ella's role in the book is to teach you a life lesson to never give up." Katerina had moved from character to theme, which was a good thing—but it was another one of those examples of kids coming up with clichéd big ideas, like "always be honest" or "be yourself." I felt like she could go deeper, and met with her again to revise her project.

Third Project, November 13: I went in with a plan to nudge Katerina to think more about theme, or at least connect her character work to some bigger ideas—but of course wanted it to come from her. Fortunately, she rose to the occasion. Here's how it went:

> ***Jamie:*** *So, the last time we met we discussed how authors make choices about the characters in a book. They assign roles and each character plays a part. Will you tell me about some of the things you've been thinking?*

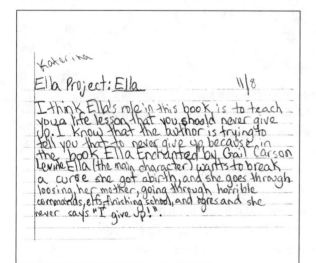
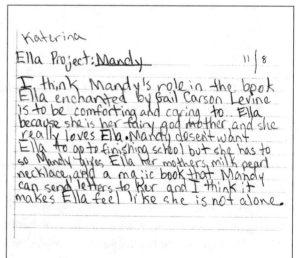

Figures 1.7a and 1.7b Katerina's Second Project: Thinking about character's roles in *Ella Enchanted*

Katerina: I think that Ella's role in the book is to teach you a lesson to never give up.

Jamie: Can you say more about that?

Katerina: Ella wants to break the curse from her fairy. She has to obey everything that people say to her. She really wants to break that curse, and she never gives up, even though she goes through ogres, elves, a long walking distance, and finishing school.

Jamie: Sounds like you found several places in the book to show this big idea. I'm noticing you are thinking about theme. Have you heard that word before?

Katerina: Why the author wrote the book?

Jamie: Right. Authors sometimes want to convey a lesson or an idea. Usually it's a message about the world, or something they want us to learn about ourselves. What's interesting about the books you are reading now is that, unlike what you read in younger grades, sometimes there are several themes. There is often one that jumps out, that is really obvious, like "never give up." But authors are tricky and don't only give you obvious themes; they also put in ideas you have to do more work to find. Is there anything popping into your head right now that could be a hidden theme?

Katerina: Not to be afraid of small problems, like being in finishing school. This is a small problem that Ella found her way out of. And there are probably more.

Jamie: Interesting. Would you like to do a project where you look for others?

Katerina: Yes, definitely. I could find at least three.

Jamie: Great. So your project is going to be to find the hidden themes. Whenever you find one, jot it down and write a few words about which parts made you think that. This is going to help you as a reader because in books like this you want to be sure you aren't just finding the obvious message. It'll help you practice reading closely to find all those themes, which is important to do as books get harder. And then you can take those messages into your life.

I was really excited about how this turned out. Katerina naturally moved toward thinking about theme. It seemed like the project about character's roles might have pushed her in that direction. I am learning that Katerina is willing to think more deeply about something, even when the strategy is new to her (see Figures 1.8a and 1.8b).

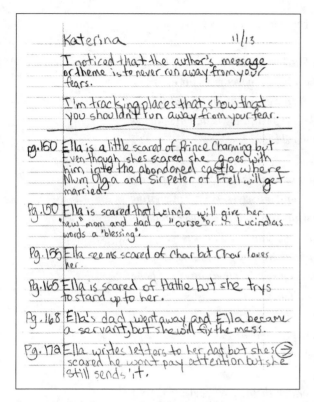
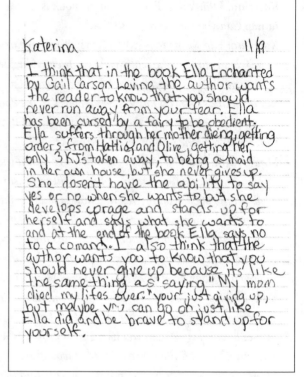

Figures 1.8a and 1.8b Katerina's multiple-theme project on *Ella Enchanted*. At the beginning of her reflection, she brings in a second theme: "don't run away from your fear."

December

What's happening in the classroom: Our conversations about tracking ideas continued, and in response to Katerina's recent work (as well as some other students in the class), many whole-class lessons centered on the idea of theme.

Now that the projects were an integral part of the reading work, we shifted and spent some time teaching different ways to record our thinking about nonfiction texts. We opted to hold off on nonfiction reading projects until students felt more comfortable with these strategies. We used short, high-interest articles to teach students a three-column structure for note-taking: idea/evidence/reflection.

Students were responsible for keeping up with their fiction reading independently as well; we gave them separate time during the day to maintain this work and continue with independent projects.

Katerina's Work: Between Thanksgiving, Christmas, and the time spent on nonfiction note-taking, Katerina's project work took a back seat during this time. Nonetheless, I was happy to see that she continued to think about the idea of hidden themes in her independent reading. Katerina made it through *Sees Behind Trees*, a book about a visually impaired Native American boy, before I got a chance to meet with her again. She wrote in her notebook, "I'm tracking places that show everyone has a hidden talent."

Fourth Project, December 9: I began by asking Katerina about her work with *Sees Behind Trees* and how she arrived at the idea of hidden talents. "Walnut, the main character, starts out blind," she explained, "and has trouble doing stuff. Then his mom finds things where he can hear, or really *see*, with his ears, instead of looking with his eyes." I was curious to know how it felt for her to do this work on her own.

> *Jamie: So you've read a whole book without us meeting. How did it go? I wasn't there to ask you questions or support you. Did thinking about theme help you understand this book better?*
>
> *Katerina: Kinda. When I was reading I just needed to find something, anything.*
>
> *Jamie: Say more about that.*
>
> *Katerina: With the project, we had already decided what to focus on. Without one, it was up to me to focus on anything I found in the book.*
>
> *Jamie: When you were free to think about anything, did some things pop out as more important than others?*
>
> *Katerina: Well, yes. Around the tenth page, I started thinking about the idea that everyone has a hidden talent. That seemed like the most important.*
>
> *Jamie: Can you say more about that?*
>
> *Katerina: Walnut can see with his ears by listening to things. It was surprising, so I thought it was important.*
>
> *Jamie: Interesting. It sounds like you are saying that if you want to get at the important theme, you should pay attention to parts that seem surprising or unusual. Like you wouldn't expect someone to see with their ears.*

> *Katerina: Yes, if it is unusual and also important, then you should pay attention to it. It has to be a combination of the two.*

From there we got to an interesting teaching point, more about prioritizing than theme: Readers need to be able to tell the difference between things that are surprising and important, and things that are surprising and *not* so important. Katerina and I agreed that she would track this idea in her next book, *Charlie and the Great Glass Elevator*. For the first six chapters, she used one color sticky note for parts that were surprising and important, and another color for parts that were surprising and *un*important (see Figure 1.9).

This project was a mixed success. Katerina created a chart in her notebook and organized the surprising/important sticky notes and surprising/unimportant sticky notes into two columns. I'm not sure how she determined which parts were important or unimportant. I'm thinking that Katerina might need to work on determining importance, but I'm not completely sure based on only one project. I'm also not sure if she was ready to move away from the idea of theme, which had really been exciting to her. I need to be careful to make sure that she feels like each project comes from *her*, otherwise it won't feel authentic and she won't be invested in it. Nonetheless, coming up with a new idea to track independently was a big step—and it was important for me to get the information about her prioritizing.

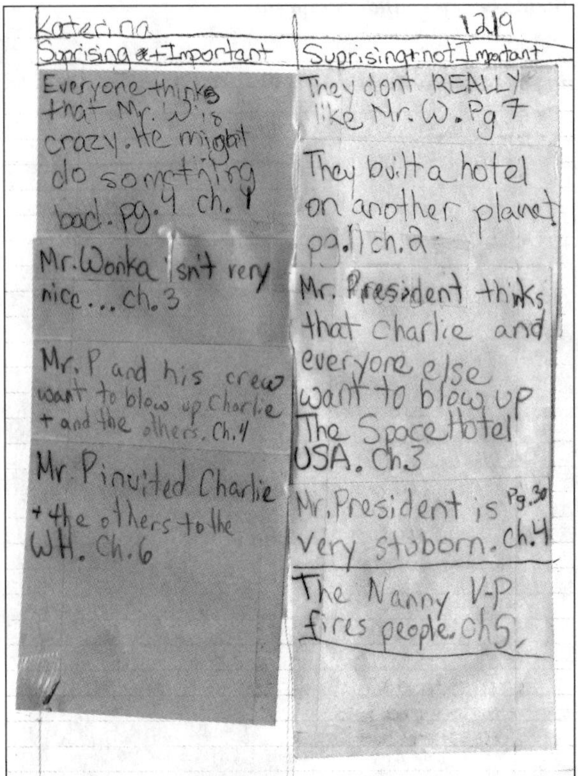

In her next book, *Which Witch?* she independently went back to looking for multiple themes, tracking evidence for two ideas: "You shouldn't change yourself for someone, unless you really love them," and "You should always be proud and believe in who you are." I guess I was right about her wanting to continue exploring theme!

In mid-December, she started reading *The Cricket in Times Square*. At first I was disappointed to see Katerina reverting back to basic questions and predictions, not a lot about theme (see Figure 1.10). Then I realized it was because the book was significantly harder than what she was used to, and that sometimes kids need to go back to simpler thinking for a while when they are getting used to new challenges in more difficult texts.

Figure 1.9 Surprising and important and surprising and not important sticky notes, divided into two columns

January/February

What's happening in the classroom: The class moved into reading historical fiction books in partnerships. We modeled taking notes using two pages side by side in the notebook; on one side, what we were learning about history, and on the other, our thoughts and ideas about the plot. Most of our modeling with the plot was around theme. We also spent a lot of time on how to deal with unfamiliar vocabulary, which was coming up a lot in the historical fiction. Because of all the whole-class work, I was unable to do many conferences for the month of January. The students were still expected to be coming up with ideas in their independent reading and tracking them.

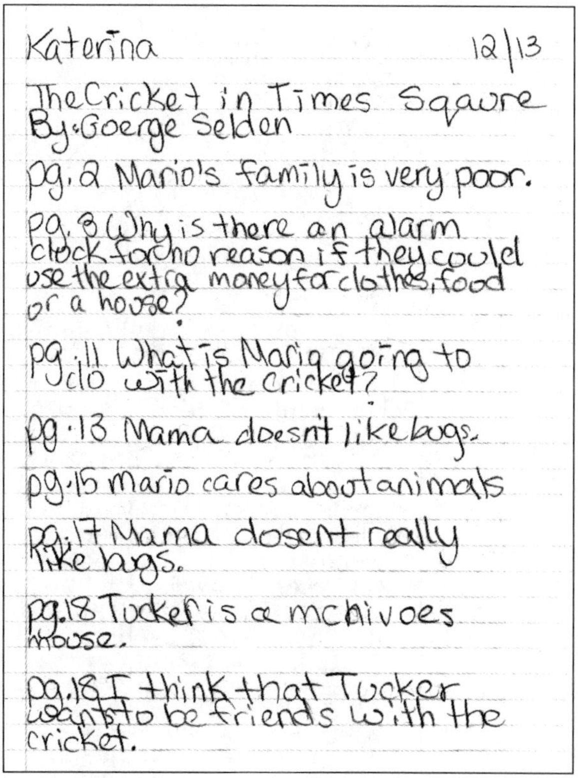
Katerina 12/13
The Cricket in Times Sqaure
By: Goerge Selden
pg. 2 Mario's family is very poor.
pg. 3 Why is there an alarm clock for no reason if they could use the extra money for clothes, food or a house?
pg. 11 What is Mario going to do with the cricket?
pg. 13 Mama doesn't like bugs.
pg. 15 mario cares aboot animals
pg. 17 Mama dosent really like bugs.
pg. 18 Tucker is a mchivoes mouse.
pg. 18 I think that Tucker wants to be friends with the cricket.

Figure 1.10 Questions and predictions on *The Cricket in Times Square*

Katerina's work: Katerina became increasingly interested in nonfiction for her independent reading during this period. A lot of her work had to do with keeping track of new information. Interestingly, she went back to thinking about important versus not-so-important surprising parts in the article "Snow on Mars," from *TIME For Kids*. ("What's most surprising? The snow is dry, like cornstarch," she wrote in her notebook on January 23; "What's most important? The snow is made of carbon dioxide.") This didn't last long, but it made me feel like maybe we could come back to the idea at some point.

Toward the end of January, Katerina went back to reading fiction. The whole-class work on informational texts and historical fiction seemed to take her in new directions. When we went back to concentrating more on the independent projects, I was curious to see what effect this work would have on her thinking.

Fifth Project, February 1: Before I had a chance to confer with her, Katerina announced that she had come up with a project on her own! She had chosen to read *Chinese Cinderella*, which seemed like a sort of middle ground between the historical fiction we'd been reading as a class and the sorts of stories she had favored earlier in the year. Interestingly, though she went back to looking at theme, some of the strategies we had worked on in class—and in earlier

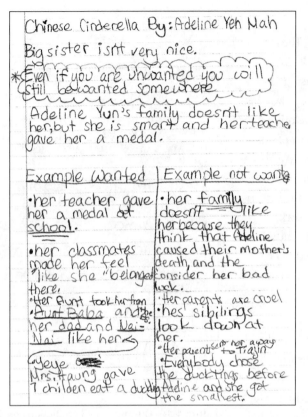

(Handwritten notebook page:)

Chinese Cinderella By: Adeline Yeh Mah

Big sister isn't very nice.

*Even if you are unwanted you will still be wanted somewhere.

Adeline Yun's family doesn't like her, but she is smart and her teacher gave her a medal.

Example Wanted	Example not wanted
• her teacher gave her a medal at school.	• her family doesn't like her because they think that Adeline caused their mother's death, and they consider her bad luck.
• her classmates made her feel like she "belonged" there.	• Her parents are cruel
• Her aunt took her from Aunt Baba and her dad and Nai Nai like her	• hes sibilings look down at her.
• Yeye & Mrs. Huang gave 7 children eat a duckling	• Her parents sent her away to Tianjin
	• Everybody chose the ducklings before Adeline and she got the smallest.

Figure 1.11 Katerina came up with this idea table by herself, influenced by whole-class lessons and past conference projects.

conferences—informed her new thinking.

"I made an idea table!" she told me excitedly. "It felt like the most important idea in this book was that even if you are unwanted, you will still be wanted somewhere. So I made a chart with examples of times Adeline was unwanted, and next to it, times when she *was* wanted. Putting them together, you can see that even though it was hard for her, the author is showing us that there were two sides to what she went through" (see Figure 1.11).

I was struck by the way she had taken the two-category sorting idea we had used in our historical fiction work, combined it with the surprising/important and surprising/unimportant assignment, and come up with a similar sort of chart to illustrate her own idea.

Mid-year reflections on Katerina: It feels as if the independent projects and the whole-class work are connecting in exciting ways for Katerina. She started the year mostly asking questions, then thinking about character, and then went through more and more sophisticated ideas about theme. Over the past several months, Katerina has become much more independent in her thinking about books. It seems clear that going back and forth between whole-class assignments and exploring her own ideas is resulting in not only deeper work, but also more independence. Katerina is becoming more self-sufficient as a reader!

Coming Up with Your Own Ideas

Even if you are on the right track, you will get run over if you just sit there.
—Will Rogers

We're Always Keeping Track of Some Line of Thinking

Back in 2005, *The Girl with the Dragon Tattoo* was at the top of the bestseller list. You could see the Day-Glo® yellow and orange cover of this racy mystery novel on buses and subways, and overhear people discussing it at water coolers and in restaurants. A closet mystery fan myself, I succumbed to temptation and picked up a copy. Complex text? Not really. But it was fairly long, with a number of twists, time shifts, and names that were difficult to pronounce. My interest was piqued.

The story began by introducing a rich old man who receives a flower in the mail once a year. No one murdered, nothing stolen. *So how is this a mystery?* I wondered; it certainly didn't start off like one. For the first ten to twenty pages I continued searching for a crime. After a while (*at last!*), a missing person. Then further in, a murder or two. *A-ha*, I thought, *now it's beginning to feel familiar—and now I'm no longer interested in looking for how it is or isn't like a mystery*. But by that point, I'd become fascinated with the relationship between the journalist Blomkvist and Lisbeth, the title character. For the next hundred pages or so I kept track of where this was going, changing my ideas every chapter or so. Were they falling in love? Did I think they should? Was it a healthy relationship? (*We children of psychiatrists are cursed with such thoughts.*) At a certain point, as the crimes and murders picked up, the relationship took a back seat in my thinking. It became more interesting to try to figure out the identity of the culprit, and like a good mystery reader, I searched for clues. At the same time, it had become clear that there was a disturbing subplot, or theme, which had been hinted at all along. I began thinking about society's tolerance of abuse toward women and how it manifests in places you don't expect.

The point here is not to recap the plot of a bestseller, but rather to show that from beginning to end of *The Girl with the Dragon Tattoo* I was always thinking about *something*. Along the way, my ideas would change, be affirmed, get discarded, or just plain stopped being interesting. Nonetheless, whenever I picked up the book there was always *some* theory, or question, or idea, that I was keeping track of and checking in on.

This sort of keeping track is not just something we do to get through popular mysteries. In order to sustain comprehension and stay interested in longer and more complex texts, most readers go through some version of the following three-step process:

- First, we **notice** something worth thinking about.
- Then, we **keep track** of it as we read.
- Periodically, we stop to **reflect** on it. We think about what we have learned, we make connections, change, or add to our original idea. And sometimes we discard our line of thinking and replace it with a different, more interesting one. Whichever way it goes, our ideas at the end are not the same as our ideas at the beginning.

This last step is the biggest shift for most student readers. Children seldom realize that they are responsible not just for *thinking* as they read, but also for their thoughts changing and developing along the way.

So if this is what a skilled reader does in his or her head to make meaning—if it is in fact an authentic, independent reading experience—it follows that a teacher would want to spend time in reading class teaching students these steps.

So how do we get this notion across to elementary or middle school children? It's not unreasonable to tell a ten-year-old, or even a seven-year-old, "Now that you are in fifth grade (or second, or seventh), you will be expected to do *two* types of reading work. On one hand, there are the things that everyone is expected to learn by the end of the year; these are what we cover in our whole-class and small group reading lessons. At the same time, all of us have interesting thoughts, and it is important that some of the work we do in reading class should come from the kids and not just the teacher. So aside from our regular lessons, each student will *also* be responsible for noticing things as they read—coming up with his or her own ideas. You will be keeping track of these ideas as you read, and thinking about how they change or grow. Your idea at the end of the book should not be exactly the same as it was at the beginning of the book. Some of the work we do in class will be *this* kind of work; and of course I will be helping you learn how to do it" (see Figure 2.1).

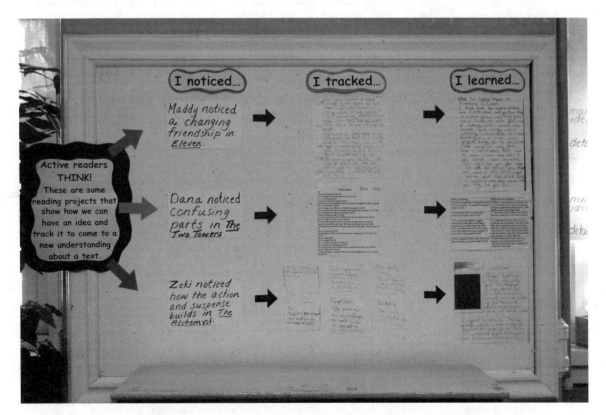

Figure 2.1 A bulletin board display in Joanne Searle's fifth-grade classroom, illustrating the idea that students are expected to notice things as they read, keep track of them, and think about what they have learned. Note the three examples of students working on very different types of things. This sends the message that such individual work can take many forms.

Articulating this at the beginning of the school year sends a message that students are *always* supposed to be thinking independently as they read. Indeed, the more often we remind children of this and celebrate their efforts, the greater the ownership they feel of their own comprehension. And, not inconsequentially, the more likely they will be to carry over these habits of mind to their whole-class curriculum and "regular" reading lessons. "There's the regular curriculum, which is basically the end-of-the-year expectations for the grade in reading, and then there's the work of the conference-based reading projects," explains fifth-grade teacher Lauren Brown, who teaches at PS 234 in New York City. "I always try to make the connection between the two very explicit. It's like lifting weights. I may be teaching you about, let's say symbolism. So we practice our symbolism muscles in a whole-class lesson, and it may not feel as exciting as when I sit down with you and say, 'What are you thinking about, what are you on about?' But those what-are-you-on-about conversations are going to go better when your muscles are stronger. It's what artists do, it's what musicians do, it's what athletes do—we work on our muscles. But kids can't *always* be doing that. Sometimes they just have to play. Otherwise how do you know they really understand when to use what you've taught them?"

Once these dual priorities are set however, the big question still remains: *What is the teacher's role in teaching children to recognize, name, and extend their own ideas?* When we teach the content of comprehension, students learn the necessary vocabulary. In this other type of instruction, we coach them in applying it to their own thinking. This means listening to what they have to say about the books they are reading and helping them *name* it.

The Power of Naming

He said true things, but called them by wrong names.
—Elizabeth Barrett Browning

For an activity to be authentic, it must have a clear purpose. Most important, it should feel meaningful to the student. When a reading activity is based on a student's own thinking, it follows that his or her level of engagement goes way up. The trouble is, many children have difficulty recognizing their own ideas, let alone articulating or building on them.

Then there's the issue of quality control. *Which lines of thinking are worth keeping track of? Which ones can we think long about, and which fail to sustain our interest? Which will help us understand more deeply?*

Having conversations about books is clearly an authentic reading activity. But not all conversations are created equal. Some teacher talk can have the undesired effect of actually inhibiting independence (Keene 2012). On the flip side, there are ways to talk with children about books so they learn to develop their own lines of thinking.

Perhaps the most critical role a teacher can play when discussing a book is to help students *name* what they are thinking about. "Noticing and naming is a central part of being a communicating human being," Peter Johnston reminds us, "but it is also crucial to becoming capable in particular activities. . . . Once we start noticing certain things, it is difficult not to notice them again" (Johnston 2004).

The power of naming is not something that applies just to reading comprehension. Psychologists have known for years that when children are able to find the right words to describe their emotions, they are more able to control them independently. Marc Brackett's social-emotional work at Yale speaks of the importance of the RULER approach, teaching kids to recognize, understand, label, express, and regulate their feelings (Brackett, Rivers, and Salovey 2011). Neurologists and cognitive scientists have studied the phenomenon as well. Matthew Lieberman at UCLA has even found evidence that labeling emotions actually regulates brain activity so that we experience "diminished responses to negative emotional images" (Lieberman et al. 2007). On the cognitive side, Sophia Jacques has written about the importance of labeling in helping children to become more flexible and sophisticated in their thinking (Jacques and Zelazo 2005).

The evidence is clear. Learning to label, or *name*, ideas and feelings helps us regulate them and be more flexible in our thinking. It follows that if we want students to be more independent and in control of their reading comprehension, they need to learn to recognize, name, and extend their own ideas.

That said, to draw out a young reader on what they are thinking as they read is not always easy. Most of us have difficulty resisting the temptation to take over the conversation. With the best of intentions, we suggest specific things to think about—often good ideas that are appropriate to the child and the situation.

Years ago, as a fourth-grade teacher, my students taught me a valuable lesson about resisting this temptation. As in many upper elementary classrooms, my daily read-aloud was from a chapter book with a lot of big ideas to talk about, since part of the point was to give students opportunities to flex their comprehension muscles. One of the best loved was Natalie Babbitt's provocative novel *Tuck Everlasting*.

The storyline of the book follows the Tucks, a family who has inadvertently drunk from a spring that stops them from growing older.

Each is frozen at a certain age; Jesse, one of the sons, is forever seventeen years old. The novel raises deep questions about growing older, death, and (most significantly) whether it would be a good or a bad thing to live forever. Along the way, a subplot develops centered on a young girl, Winnie, who falls into a relationship with Jesse.

For several days, my nine-year-old readers talked animatedly about the story. The trouble was, the only thing they wanted to discuss was the relationship between Winnie and Jessie. *Should she drink from the spring and be with him forever? Was he being too pushy about it? What about her family?* This went on for a week or so, with many individual opinions entering the mix. After a while, fearing they were missing the larger point, I stepped in and suggested that today's conversation should focus instead on whether or not it would be a good thing to live forever. After all, that was the point of the book, wasn't it?

My students agreed to try it. Stefon was the first to voice an idea. "I think it would be cool to live forever," he volunteered. "Actually, it might be sad," Margo responded. "You'd watch all your friends die and then you'd be alone." A couple of others haltingly agreed with one point of view or another, followed by a lengthy pause. Finally, Allison broke the silence, bringing the conversation back to what all the students were clearly thinking about. "Now about Winnie and Jesse . . ." she began. And they were off and running.

Listening as my readers continued to build on their lines of thinking, I had to acknowledge that in this moment it really didn't matter whether they talked about what I considered important. In fact, altering the already productive flow of conversation could feel like I was correcting them. What mattered was that the students had come up with their own ideas about the book and that these ideas were evolving as they continued to read. Kids referred back to things others had said, they argued and built on one another's thinking, and they cited evidence from the text. Whether my students walked away from *Tuck Everlasting* with ideas about living forever was less important than learning to connect and follow a big idea over time.

In *The Art of Teaching Writing*, Lucy Calkins cautions teachers to "teach the writer, not the writing." In other words, what students learn from one piece of writing that they bring to the next is more important than perfecting any one piece. Similarly, for an elementary or middle school reader, it is often more important to *teach the reader, not the book.*

To be sure, giving students a new idea to think about is not a bad thing; it may increase their repertoire of ways to look at a text or introduce a new lens for thinking. But when a teacher consistently jumps in and makes the decision of what to think about, young readers do not learn how to make such decisions themselves. Moreover, they learn to wait for the adult to hint at the "right" answer, rather than taking a chance on voicing an idea that may be different from what the teacher wants.

So what does a teacher do instead? In math, we want students to be able to look at a problem, weigh the variables, and decide on the most efficient problem-solving strategy for *that* problem.

Reading may be approached as a similar sort of process. Skilled readers have a repertoire of ways to think about texts and make decisions of which ones to call upon, based on the demands of a particular book or article. To do this well, students need to have a repertoire to begin with—and they need to have the confidence to believe that their own ideas are worth thinking about.

One of the most powerful things we can do for our young readers is to help them realize they are capable of coming up with valid ideas on their own. This means listening to what they have to say and helping them name it in a way that is bigger than any one book. The important thing is that they take away something they can bring to the next book, and the book after that.

The irony here is that the usual tendency is to push students to always be more specific. Most of the time this makes a lot of sense. We certainly don't want readers thinking vague thoughts that are not grounded in the actual text. On the other hand, when our objective is to teach something that will be generalizable to other reading experiences, beyond today's book, we need to start with specifics—but then pull back to name the idea in a general way that could apply to other texts as well. A student may express that it is unfair for Jesse to pressure Winnie to drink from the spring, that he is only looking out for himself. And a teacher may respond, "It sounds as if you are thinking about the reasons characters in books do the things they do—and whether you agree with their actions or not." Now the specific idea about *Tuck Everlasting* is identified as something the student can think about in just about any narrative.

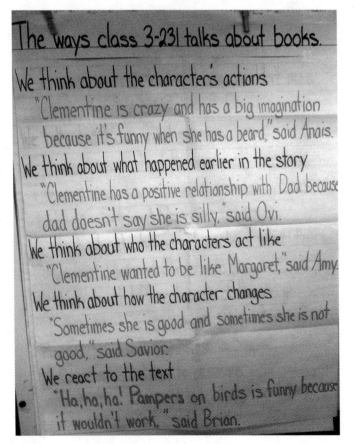

Sometimes the more sophisticated thinking happens not when we go *from the general to the specific*, but *from the specific to the general* (see Figure 2.2). And this is what we are after as we help students name the ideas they are coming up with as they read.

Figure 2.2 A third-grade chart from PS 142, on the Lower East Side of New York City. The teacher has listened to specific ideas the students voiced about the class read-aloud and named them in more general ways—so that they can be applied to the next book, and the book after that. The idea is to *teach the reader, not the book*.

Since learning to recognize one's own ideas is different for every reader, it makes sense that much of this work should happen in individual reading conferences. Students in elementary and middle school are still concrete thinkers, just beginning to understand ideas in a more abstract way. It makes sense, then, that as their thinking deepens and becomes more independent, these conferences should end with specific, tangible work for each student to do. Assigning students specific work to practice a comprehension strategy helps them concretize it, retain it, and hopefully carry it to their future reading. In the end, we want to enable readers *to think about a text when no one is telling them what to think about.*

To do this work well, it is important to first be clear on what an individual, conference-based reading project is—and what it is *not*.

Rethinking the Individual Reading Project

Anyone can make the simple complicated.
Creativity is making the complicated simple.
— Charles Mingus, jazz bassist and composer

Understanding What a Conference-Based Reading Project Is *Not*

The term "reading projects" conjures visions of dioramas, posters, and shoeboxes, and (often) work that looks suspiciously like it was done by parents. In the end, we get a product that may be beautiful to look at, but does little to make the child a better reader. Worse, all those hours spent choosing the right marker or the most attractive font takes time away from *actual reading*. If we accept Allington's assertion that "Kids need to read a lot if they are to become good readers" (2006), it follows that any activity they spend time on in reading class—other than reading—had better be worth it.

So what is the difference between conference-based reading projects and those more traditionally assigned in reading classrooms? Probably the most common work assigned to children learning to read is answering questions from a teacher or a program. While skillful questioning is certainly important, true comprehension instruction involves students coming up with—and extending—their *own* ideas.

It's not as if the importance of students tracking their individual thinking has gone unrecognized. In many classrooms, students jot their thoughts on sticky notes as they read and stick them on the relevant page. This has the dual advantage of providing the reader with a concrete way to record and connect his or her thoughts, as well as giving the teacher a window into what the child is or isn't understanding (Tovani 2011). The problem is that in many classes students get carried away, to put it mildly. Some readers end up with more sticky notes than pages in the book they are reading. Consequently, their thinking becomes unfocused or lost entirely.

A conference-based reading project prioritizes students' emerging thinking and helps them focus on a particular idea. It not only pushes them to go deeper, but also gives them work to do to practice following and extending a line of thinking.

Much has been written about the importance of talk in teaching comprehension strategies. Peter Johnston (2004, 2012), Maria Nichols (2008), and Ellin Keene (2012) all make convincing cases for the essential role of conversation and carefully crafted oral language in helping children learn to understand. Conference-based reading projects should not be prioritized over ongoing booktalks in classrooms. In fact, the work assigned in this sort of conference is an outgrowth of a conversation between teacher and student. Still, the fact is that most schools expect students to produce some sort of writing in response to text as an integral part of their reading instruction. Such work certainly gives a teacher a window into a child's comprehension, and it allows for ongoing assessment. But if the only purpose of a reading project is for the *teacher* to get smarter, it is not a good enough reason. To justify the time spent away from actual reading, the work should also help students deepen their comprehension—and hopefully add to their repertoire of ways to look at and understand the texts they read. A conference-based reading project must be as useful for the student as it is for the teacher.

With this in mind, reading class need not be the place where students spend time crafting a formal piece of writing in response to a text. Learning to write well about reading is important, but it's more appropriately done in writing workshop. The sort of writing about reading we assign in a conference-based reading project is not necessarily polished or neat—it is writing that helps a reader *understand*.

These projects should *not* be

    a.) primarily about answering teacher generated questions

    b.) formal writing about reading

    c.) solely for the purpose of giving teachers something to assess

    d.) work that takes a lot of time away from actual reading.

Rather, a conference-based reading project should be redefined as quick and dirty, informal writing about reading that

a.) helps students recognize and develop their own ideas about what they are reading

b.) gives students opportunities to learn, practice, and internalize specific comprehension strategies

c.) gives teachers a window into their students' understanding

d.) doesn't take too much time away from actual reading.

So what does a conference-based reading project look like? And how might such a conference unfold?

Naomi and Sophie: One Conference-Based Reading Project

Naomi, a student in Sophie Brady's fifth-grade class, is an enthusiastic reader. She especially loves fantasy, realistic fiction, and biography—almost anything with strong characters. Though assessments showed her to be right on grade level, Sophie had a nagging feeling that her student could be doing more. "Naomi's sticky notes and reading notebook have lots of *beginnings* of ideas, but she never seems to follow up on anything," her teacher observed. "It's like she thinks about one idea, jots quick notes, then jumps to another. The same thing happens in partner booktalks; she jumps from one thing to the next when she talks as well. She has some good thoughts—the next step is to get her to elaborate on her ideas."

In thinking ahead about a conference-based reading project for Naomi, Sophie knew that getting her to come up with an initial idea was not likely to be a problem. The priority would be to work on following an idea over time, seeing how it evolves or changes. Hopefully getting Naomi to practice this through an individual assignment would start her on the road to making it a habit—and ultimately deepen her comprehension. But what sort of idea should she follow?

As Sophie approached her in early October, Naomi was about a third of the way through *The London Eye Mystery* by Siobhan Dowd. Sophie began with an open-ended question, rather than asking for a retell.

> **Sophie:** *So Naomi, you're reading The London Eye Mystery. What have you been thinking about in this book so far?*
> **Naomi:** *Ted and Kat are brother and sister, and they are arguing a lot.*
> **Sophie:** *Can you say more about that?*

Naomi: *Well, Ted is a rule follower and Kat is a rebel. So they are different and don't always get along.*

Sophie: *Do you think this is just typical sibling fighting? Or is there something more there?*

Naomi: *Well, I think it has to do with the book being a mystery. They are trying to find out what happened to their cousin who got on but never got off the London Eye. So they are each good at different things.*

Sophie: *Say more about that.*

Naomi: *Ted is good with facts, and Kat is good with people. But Ted is awful with people. So it's like she's good at what he's not, and vice versa.*

Let's stop and look at the teaching moves so far in this conference. True to form, Naomi's first thought has to do with the characters, her usual, go-to topic. Sophie goes with it, but pushes Naomi further, asking, "Can you say more about that?" Naomi gives more detail, but Sophie continues to ask her to think harder about her initial idea: "Do you think this is just typical sibling fighting? Or is there something more there?" Finally, the third time around, Naomi's thinking moves to something deeper; she is still talking about character traits, but she's also considering what the character traits have to do with the way the story will unfold ("I think it has to do with the book being a mystery"). Sophie *continues* to push, asking to her to say more yet again. Now Naomi's idea is not only more specific ("Ted is good with facts, and Kat is good with people"), but she has begun to come up with her own interpretation ("So it's like she's good at what he's not, and vice versa").

As simple as it may seem, Sophie has made some decisive moves in this short exchange. For one thing, she does not try to move Naomi away from her go-to topic, character, but rather pushes her to go deeper in her thinking. Ellin Keene (2012) points out that as adults, the first thing we say is seldom our best thinking. The same is true with children—and yet as teachers, when we let students express an idea of their own, we tend to quickly jump in with our own agenda. By pushing Naomi to say more about her first idea, and then say more again, Sophie gets her beyond a surface-level observation and on to something more.

Where to go from here? Back to the conference:

Sophie: *It sounds like you are thinking about what skill each character brings to the story, or in this case, to the solving of the mystery.*

Naomi: *Yeah, I think each of the characters is going to help in their own way to solve the mystery. It'll be like teamwork.*

Sophie: *Let me see if I am getting this right. You're thinking about how the different personalities of the characters will come together as the plot develops, like a jigsaw puzzle.*

Naomi: *Right.*

Sophie: *What you are doing here is really important work, Naomi. You are always really good at thinking about characters. As books get harder though, a reader has to think about how the combination of different characters and their personalities go together—and how that combination will affect the story. It's a very sophisticated type of prediction and something you can do in other books besides this one!*

Naomi: *Cool.*

Here is the hard part. Once a student has expressed an idea about what they are reading, the job of the teacher is to step back and name the strategy as something that can be used beyond today's book. Sophie put together Naomi's comments and made a generalization about the type of thing she is doing as a reader. This teaching point becomes the basis of the student's reading project. Again, especially in elementary and middle school, we want to *teach the reader, not the book.*

The next step is to make this kid-developed teaching point the basis of the work the student will be assigned after the conversation—her conference-based reading project.

Sophie: *So here's something I'd like you to do to work on this skill. Jot down parts where a character helps to solve the mystery. This could be Kat or Ted, but I imagine in a book of this length, there are other characters too who will contribute.*

Naomi: *Yeah, there's the aunt, their mom, and their dad, too. And they all have things they are good at, too.*

Sophie: *Great, so pay attention to different places where a character's personality helps them get closer to finding their cousin. What do you think would be the best way to keep track of these jottings?*

Naomi: *Well . . . I could use sticky notes. Oh! I could use one color for Kat, one for Ted, and then assign the other characters colors too. Then, when I'm done, it will be easy to see who helped solve the mystery and how.*

Sophie: *And once you've finished, look over your sticky notes and write a few lines in your reader's notebook about how the characters' personalities combined to solve the mystery. Do you think you can get this done by Thursday?*

Naomi: *(excited) Yes. This should be interesting!*

Sophie: *Doing this work will help you practice thinking about how the different personalities of characters go together to make things happen in a story. That's something that will help you understand any book with characters better, not just* The London Eye Mystery!

The assignment Naomi is left with is clear. It has a due date and specific expectations. As assigned, it shouldn't take too much time away from her reading. Important too is the fact that after going over the logistics of the project, Sophie was careful to repeat the teaching point a second time at the end of the conference. The reason for this has to do with human nature. The last thing we hear in any conversation is often the thing that looms largest in our memory. Doesn't it make sense, then, for our parting shot to be the most important teaching point, rather than procedural stuff about which sticky notes to use or how many pages to read?

Three days later, Naomi turned in the work she had done. After collecting and looking over her sticky notes, she expressed her thinking in the form of a recipe: "How to Solve a Mystery."

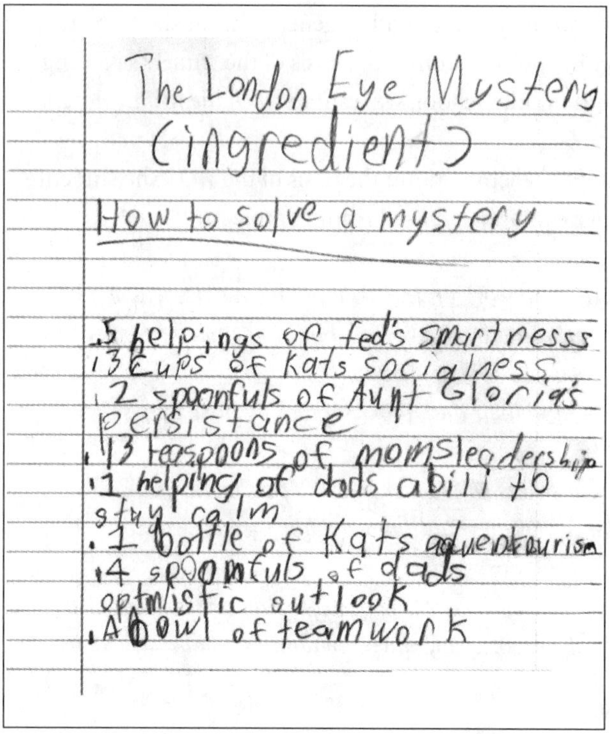
The London Eye Mystery
(ingredients)
How to solve a mystery
.5 helpings of ted's smartnesss
13 cups of Kats socialness
2 spoonfuls of Aunt Gloria's persistance
13 teaspoons of moms leadership
1 helping of dads abili to stay calm
1 bottle of Kats adventurism
4 spoomfuls of dads optmistic outlook
A bowl of teamwork

Figure 3.1 Naomi's Recipe for "How to Solve a Mystery"

Not only did Naomi create her own format (a recipe, see Figure 3.1) to showcase her thinking, she was able to follow and develop her idea throughout the book, which was Sophie's initial goal. In addition, she showed that she was able to identify character traits independently (intelligent, social, persistent, ability to lead, etc.). "This makes me think I can work with Naomi to explore ideas other than characters," Sophie commented afterward. "Next conference, I may push her to look at theme, or setting—it's time she started moving away from only ever thinking about character."

Understanding What a Conference-Based Reading Project *Is*

Although a conference-based reading project is based on a student's thinking, the teacher plays an important role in helping to recognize, name, and extend that thinking. The trick is to match individual students with appropriate work to do that will make them better readers, and to do so in such a way that they buy in and feel excited.

Most people are more invested in a task when they feel a sense of ownership. For this reason, we want the lines of thinking students explore in their projects to be their own. This is easier said than done; many children aren't even aware that they are having thoughts as they read, let alone be able to name what they are, or tell a big idea from a small one. The teacher's role is to help them recognize the ideas they are having, and how to extend them in order to come up with new understandings. "I am not in their heads, nor should I be in their heads," reflects Joanne Searle, a fifth-grade teacher at Manhattan New School. "I have to take what they're starting out with and help them shape a project that grows their own thinking."

As with any effective pedagogy, it is always a good idea to let kids know what is expected on *their* end as well. Once they are used to this sort of conference, some of the responsibility for coming up with an assignment may be given over to the student. From the reader/student's point of view, coming up with a conference-based reading project may be thought of in three steps:

1. *Notice* something in the text that you find interesting—and talk about it! For example
   - what a character is like, or what she does
   - something you agree (or disagree with)
   - something you like (or don't like) about the way the author wrote it
   - a part that seems especially important.

2. *Keep track* of it as you read, and see how your idea grows or changes. Use
   - sticky notes
   - graphic organizers
   - reading notebooks
   - margin notes.

3. Look back and (briefly!) record your thinking. Once you are done, *sum up* what you think. You might do this by
   - writing a few sentences
   - choosing a few sticky notes that go together and writing a few lines about why

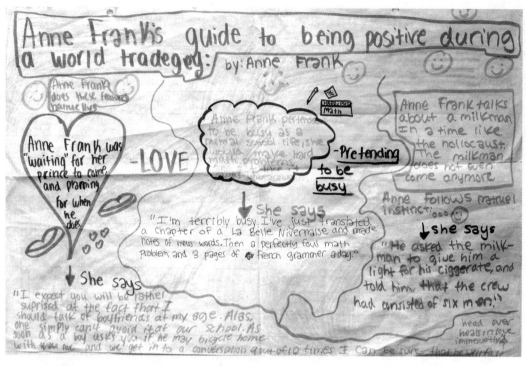

Figure 3.2 Anne Frank's guide to being positive during a world tradegey [*sic*]

- making a timeline
- making a diagram, web, or some other graphic organizer. (See Figures 3.2 and 3.3 for some rather elaborate examples!)

The teacher's primary job in a reading conference is to help the student recognize and name his or her own idea. To do this well, we must develop our own ability to *listen for and name* what children are noticing and thinking about as they read—in a way that is *bigger than just the one book*. If a student is retelling the plot of a Judy Blume book and commenting on Peter's complicated relationship with Fudge, a teacher might point out that he or she is paying attention to places where a main character seems to be feeling opposite things—an important thing to do in *any* narrative text.

It is important for the teacher to differentiate the *teaching point* from the *assignment*, or *project*. The project is the work the student does with a specific text. The teaching point is the larger, generalizable strategy—bigger than the current book—that the student is expected to take to the next book, and the book after that. In Naomi's case, the assignment was to pay attention to different places where a character's personality helps to solve the mystery. The larger aim—the *teaching point*—was to think about how the different personalities of characters go together in any narrative, and how this combination affects the story.

The assignment is something Sophie will collect from Naomi and respond to, as she does with any classwork or homework assignment. The *teaching point* is what she will return to in the next conference and what Sophie expects Naomi to be thinking about in her next book. Carl Anderson (2001) has immortalized the phrase "How's it going?" as the starting point for a good writing conference—but this does not mean that every conference starts with a tabula rasa. Once a teacher gets to know her students, it is fair to make them accountable for holding on to what she taught them last time around and to start the conference by checking in. When Sophie next meets with Naomi, she may begin with, "How's it going, noticing the way different characters' personalities combine to affect the story?" In this way, she sends the message that the teaching point from the last conference is something Naomi should be thinking about from now on—not just in *The London Eye Mystery*.

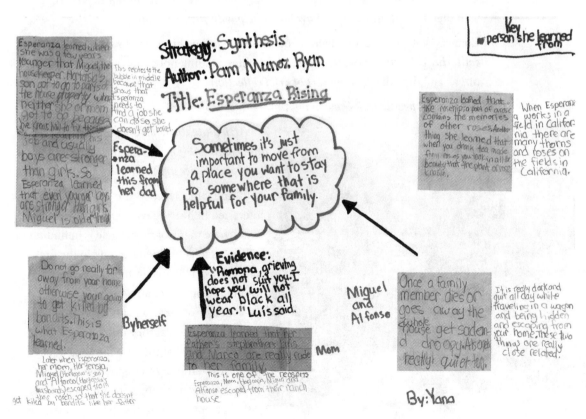

Figure 3.3 Yana's synthesis of *Esperanza Rising*

Once named, such a strategy can become the jumping-off point for an informal, targeted reading project, which students recognize came from their own noticings. Children leave the conference feeling capable of coming up with interesting thoughts about what they are reading and excited to go further in developing their own ideas.

While on the surface the conference may feel like an unstructured conversation, the teacher also follows a particular sequence of steps:

1. *"What are you thinking about (name of text)?"*

2. *Listen* for the most interesting thing the reader says or does. (*Often, this involves finding a piece of the retell that contains an idea or opinion.*)

3. Ask the reader to *say more about* that thing. Ask follow-up questions. *Jot down* specific words or phrases that you can repeat later in the conference to show you were actively listening.

4. *Name* what the reader is doing in a way that is *about more than the current book*, so it can be generalized as a strategy for future reading. *Teach* him or her to go further with this strategy and explain *how it will help with future reading*.

5. Come up with a project that allows the reader to *follow his or her line of thinking by collecting evidence in the text* (e.g., sticky notes, reading notebook, graphic organizer), and then *doing some sort of brief reflection*.

6. *Agree on a specific task (how many, how long, etc.).*

7. *Articulate the teaching point again as a final comment* (i.e., *"Doing this project will help you practice . . ."*).

By and large, teachers are people who are interested in hearing what children have to say. Where many of us struggle is in finding strategies to get students to talk in the first place. Especially in communities where children have only ever answered pre-prepared questions from teachers and programs, it is not surprising that they initially fall silent when asked what they are thinking about a text. It is tempting to leap in too quickly with our own agenda rather than help students find an entry point for expressing their own

ideas. As Lucy Calkins (1994) reminds us, "Every child has a story to tell. The question is whether they will tell it to *you*."

One way to help children elaborate on their thinking is to hold off on leaping in with our own agenda. Once a student says something—anything—the temptation is to rush in and teach. But how often is the first thing that comes out of people's mouths their best thinking? Rather

than accepting the very first words a student says, it is helpful to pick out one part of what she has said and ask her to *say more about that* (Keene 2012). But we don't want to stop there. When the student answers, pick out the most interesting part of her response and ask her to say more about *that*. Like Russian dolls, one inside the other, when a teacher continues to ask for elaboration in this way, by the third or fourth *say more about that*, the reader's thinking is almost always deeper. And *then* we can stop to name it. Though it goes against the nature of a reading conference to think too much in terms of rules, it may be helpful for a teacher who is beginning this work to force himself to ask a child to *say more* about something *at least three times* before deciding on a teaching point. With this in mind, a shorthand way of thinking about the steps in the conference would be

- "Say more about that." (*at least 3 times!*)

- Name the type of idea the student is having, using language that is about more than just the current book.

- Negotiate an assignment that will allow the reader to practice the comprehension strategy and extend his or her idea.

- End by repeating the teaching point, emphasizing how it can apply to the next book, and the book after that.

With repeated practice, even students who have a hard time discussing books begin to respond and come up with ideas for independent reading projects. "For the kids, it's hopefully teaching them the real meaning of reading, to understand and have your own thoughts," says Lauren Brown. "But bigger than that, it's teaching them that what they have to say matters. That

I don't have to say anything to you for you to have something to say, and what you have to say can be every bit as important as what's on your report card. So in a perfect world, they can name it—and in an imperfect world we help them name it, and over time they get better at naming it themselves. But either way, it's about them practicing developing their own ideas about what they're reading."

Carving out time in the day for conference-based reading projects allows us important opportunities to listen and assign our readers work that is personalized and rigorous.

Umbrella Categories

TYPES OF READING CONFERENCES AND SAMPLE PROJECTS

"At first, when I tried giving each student an individual assignment with every new conference, it was totally overwhelming," laments Jamie Kushner, a fourth-grade teacher in New York City. "It felt like I needed some sort of list, or at least a way to organize the different kinds of conferences in my head. Starting to narrow down the projects by thinking about what category they fell into helped a lot. To be honest, once I thought ahead about that, I'd sometimes listen for something the kid said that allowed me to angle it toward one category or another, depending on what I felt the kid needed to work on. So it still came from them, but I guess I kind of manipulated it, too. Anyway, it got a lot easier for me to listen to what the student had to say when I went in with ideas of what to look for."

Yetta Goodman (2002) reminds us that there are no substitutes for careful kid-watching and good listening. Nonetheless, a reading teacher can become more confident and able to adapt to new students by having umbrella categories, or types of conferences, at her fingertips.

The following nine umbrella categories are intended as a work in progress. In fact, several of them were added in meetings with teachers who said, "Nice so far, but what about *this* type of conference?" As such, it is by no means definitive. The best use of this list would be as a jumping-off point for educators to add to, revise, and refine.

Several of these conference types lend themselves more to narrative, some to informational text, and some can apply to both. My hope is that teachers will actively adapt these categories to

Types of Reading Conferences
METACOGNITIVE

- Noticing Your Own Reactions: Talking Back to Text

- Connecting the Dots: Deciding Which Parts Go Together and Which Don't

- Thinking About Your Thinking: Noticing Where It Makes Sense or Gets Confusing

- Walking in a Character's Shoes: What Would *You* Do?

TEXT-BASED

- Prioritizing: What's Important to Remember and What's OK to Forget

- What the Author Wants Us to Think About or Feel: Looking for Themes, Lessons, and Big Ideas

- Paying Attention to How Things Develop: Tracking Change or the Development of an Idea

- Compare and Contrast: Noticing What Is Similar and Different

- Reading Like a Writer: Thinking About How the Author Wrote It

their own teaching style, their own students, and their own purposes.

These types may certainly overlap; for example, it would be possible to work on connecting the dots while at the same time paying attention to how things develop in a text. Nonetheless, many teachers find it helpful to think of these categories as a starting place as they begin working with conference-based reading projects.

What follows are brief descriptions of the nine conference categories. I've included examples of sample teaching points for each, in kid-friendly language, as well as possible reading projects. They are intended as illustrations, not scripts. It's important, always, to remember that the specifics of a good conference should come from what *the individual student* says and does. With that disclaimer in mind, here we go.

Noticing Your Own Reactions: Talking Back to Text

This is among the most basic conference types and is often appropriate for struggling readers or students who have difficulty saying anything other than "what [the book] was about." The truth is, there are kids out there who aren't even aware they are *supposed* to have a thought as they read. A "Noticing Your Own Reactions" conference is just that—paying attention to (and identifying) thoughts and feelings that cross your mind as you read.

Easier Variation

Teaching Point: "Readers notice thoughts and feelings in their heads as they read. For example, some parts of the text may make us feel sad, or excited, or surprised. Some parts might make us think things as well; for example, we might disagree with a decision one of the characters makes, or believe that a fact in a nonfiction text is incorrect. It's important to stop and pay attention when we have thoughts or feelings."

PROJECT: (*Narrative/Informational*) Put sticky notes on places where you have a thought or feeling and label them (e.g., "I felt sad," "It was funny," "I disagree with what Ramona did here," "Not true—cats *don't* like milk," etc.). Afterward, look over your sticky notes and write a few lines about the types of thoughts or feelings you are having. (*Note: For more struggling readers, thoughts/feelings passages may be "coded"—for example writing "HA!" for a funny part, "!!!" for an exciting part, or "No!" for a part you disagree with, etc.*)

More Difficult Variation

Teaching Point: "It is important to understand what the author is saying, but we also want to have our own ideas. Sometimes readers argue with a text; for example, they might think something that happens in a story is unrealistic or that the author left out important information in an article. When readers disagree (or agree) with something in a text, it is important to stop and take notice."

PROJECT: (*Narrative/Informational*) Mark (and briefly explain) places where you want to argue with the text, e.g., disagree with an author's point of view in an informational text or feel that something is unrealistic in a narrative. When you are done, write a few lines summing up (and perhaps connecting) these parts.

Connecting the Dots: Deciding Which Parts Go Together and Which Don't

Beginning in second grade, our most important job as teachers of reading is to teach children to sustain comprehension over increasingly longer texts. Many students in elementary and middle school comprehend perfectly well for a page or two, but when it comes to longer chapter books they don't realize that something in chapter six connects to chapter one—especially when you add in that small detail from chapter five. Making these sorts of connections, i.e., connecting the dots, is one of the keys to understanding longer and more complicated texts.

Teaching young readers to connect the dots should start small. Sometimes it's things on the same page that go together and make a reader say "a-ha." As texts become more complex, a reader must make connections across many pages. A Connecting the Dots conference may be simple or complex; either way, it addresses one of the most fundamental comprehension strategies.

Easier Variation

Teaching Point: "To understand longer books, it's important to think about how the parts go together. In stories, sometimes an author will tell you how a character feels on one page and then more about it on the next page; the reader has to put those things together. In nonfiction, there might be a fact about what an animal eats on one page and something more about their food two pages later. Again, the reader has to connect those things in order to understand."

PROJECT: (*Narrative*) For the next two/three/however many chapters, keep track of parts that connect to tell you something about the main character's personality. When you find two passages that go together, mark them with the same color sticky note. When you are done, write a few sentences about how these parts go together and what they show you about what the character is like.

PROJECT: (*Informational*) Same as above, but keep track of facts about the things that go together.

More Difficult Variation

Teaching Point: "In order to understand harder books, readers need to connect parts that go together—but it is also important to notice when things *don't* go together. For example, in a story we might read about a character being mean and selfish, but then come across a part where he acts nice and generous. In a nonfiction text, we might read a fact about the Minutemen fighting the Redcoats in the Revolutionary War and then come across a fact about some colonists actually liking the British. When a reader comes across parts that seem to contradict each other, it is important to stop and think about what it means."

PROJECT: (*Narrative/Informational*) For each chapter or section, mark two things that seem to contradict, or go against, one another, then write a sentence about what doesn't make sense. As you continue to read, if another part helps you understand the contradiction, stop reading to jot about it.

Thinking About Your Thinking: Noticing Where It Makes Sense or Gets Confusing

Years ago, I observed a fifth-grade reading lesson with Shelley Harwayne at a school where many students were well below grade level. Although the children were well behaved and dutifully doing their work, they had difficulty talking about what they were reading—and an even harder time writing about it. "The problem is," Shelley pointed out, "that they are all so *passive*. When they don't understand something, they don't know to stop and think about it."

It's critical for readers to have a repertoire of "fix-it" strategies to repair comprehension when something is difficult to understand (Keene and Zimmermann 1997). But before we can even go there, we must teach children to notice when something doesn't make sense, and think about exactly *why* it is confusing. "We need to explicitly teach our students how to monitor their thinking while reading," Smokey Daniels (2014) reminds us.

Taking this idea one step further, over time skilled readers can become aware of the particular types of things that tend to be confusing for *them*. (On a personal note, I often lose the thread when there is too much setting description, or too many numbers!) Helping students become aware of their personal stumbling blocks, and develop strategies for how to deal with them, can be transformative for a struggling reader.

The purpose of a "Thinking About Your Thinking" conference is to reinforce the idea that as important as it is to understand, it is just as important to know when you *don't* understand.

Easier Variation

Teaching Point: "It might feel embarrassing sometimes to admit that we don't understand something we are reading. The truth is that all readers, no matter how skilled they are, sometimes come upon parts they don't understand. It is important to be aware when there is a part in a book we don't quite get, and stop to think about it."

Project: (*Narrative/Informational*) For each of the next four/five/six chapters, mark the most confusing part with a sticky note. Jot down what made it confusing. Then look across your sticky notes, and write a few sentences about what you did to understand.

More Difficult Variation

Teaching Point: "We know that all readers sometimes come to parts in books which are confusing. Most readers have particular *types* of things that are especially confusing for *them*. For example, when a story skips ahead in time, or when a lot of different characters are talking, or

when a nonfiction text has a lot of numbers in it. It is important to get to know yourself as a reader and become aware of your personal hard-to-understand parts, so that you can be especially careful to stop and think when you come upon them."

Project: (*Narrative/Informational*) For each of the next four/five/six/seven chapters, mark the most confusing parts with sticky notes and jot about what makes them difficult. Then put the sticky notes in groups. What is the same about the parts that were hard to understand? Write about your groups and why you chose to put certain sticky notes together. Is it just in this book, or are these types of things hard for you to understand in other texts as well?

For a more detailed example, see conference transcript "Places That Are Confusing," in Chapter 5.

Walking in a Character's Shoes: What Would *You* Do?

One of the most overused phrases in reading classrooms across the country is "text-to-self connection." Even Ellin Keene, who coined the phrase back in 1997, complains about how ubiquitous it has become. "I knew when I saw an actress use it on a sitcom that it had gone too far," she laments. "The problem isn't the idea itself, but the way so many schools use it without thinking."

The issue is that not all text-to-self connections are created equal. When a child is reading *Sounder* or *Old Yeller*, to say "My grandmother has a dog" may be a text-to-self connection, but it doesn't really help in understanding the book. When we teach students to make personal connections, it's critical to also teach them to make decisions about *which connections help us to understand.*

A good entry point for making useful personal connections is comparing what characters in books do, think, or feel to what we might do ourselves. A "Walking in a Character's Shoes" conference can be just the place to introduce this strategy.

Easier Variation

Teaching Point: "In order to understand stories, it is important to think about the actions, feelings, and decisions of the main characters. One way to do this is to put ourselves in their shoes and think about whether we agree or disagree with their reactions."

Project: (*Narrative*) Find *x* number of places in the book that describe a character's action, feeling, or decision. Think about whether you agree or disagree with them, and why. Jot down your thinking on a sticky note or in a notebook.

More Difficult Variation

Teaching Point: "Authors make their characters do, say, and think things for particular reasons, to make the story go a certain way. Readers may consider whether they agree with the author's decisions and whether they might have had the character do something different if they had written it themselves."

Project: (*Narrative*) Find *x* number of places in the book where the author made a character do something you strongly agree or disagree with. Jot down a line or two about *why* you think the author wrote it that way and what you would (or wouldn't) have done differently.

Prioritizing: What's Important to Remember and What's OK to Forget

Most teachers have met the student who reads a biography of Abraham Lincoln and remembers he had a beard, but forgets that he freed the slaves. Any upper elementary or middle school educator who has taught basic note-taking skills can tell you that determining importance is a significant hurdle for this age group. Although we sometimes associate prioritizing with informational texts, it is equally critical for reading narrative; a reader needs to know when a character's reaction is significant, or if a particular plot detail is important to the story.

As texts get longer, there is more and more information to process, and it becomes increasingly difficult for students to discern just which pieces of information are most important. While prioritizing is to some extent subjective—after all, if you were doing research on nineteenth-century hairstyles, Abe's beard *would* be pretty significant—more often than not, there are clues in the text itself that tip us off as to what we are supposed to remember. One of our most important jobs as teachers of reading is to help students learn how to pick up on these text-based cues.

Picking up on these text-based cues can be a daunting task for young readers, especially when they have limited knowledge of the subject or genre. Sometimes taking the opposite point of view and considering what information is *less* important can take the pressure off, and feels like a more accessible entry point for a struggling reader.

Easier and More Difficult Variations

(Narrative/Informational) See conference transcript "Important to Remember," in Chapter 5.

What the Author Wants Us to Think About or Feel: Looking for Themes, Lessons, and Big Ideas

One of the criteria most often assessed in tests of reading comprehension for elementary and middle school readers is "Main Idea." The problem is that most texts of any complexity have multiple big ideas, not just one (Keene 2012). To give students the message that there is one "right answer" is not just intimidating, it's also misleading.

That said, learning to infer (and name) themes in a text is one of the most complicated tasks facing a young reader. Although these "big ideas" are woven into the text itself, the process of uncovering them involves a lot of connecting-the-dots work; readers must identify and connect passages that speak to what the author wants us to think about, or feel. This sort of conference is one way to provide a concrete activity to help students practice identifying themes, lessons, and big ideas.

Easier Variation

Teaching Point: "Apart from just understanding what is happening in a story, there are things an author wants us to think about, or feel, at the end of the book. Readers need to pick out these big ideas, and they aren't always obvious—authors don't usually just announce, 'Here is the big idea!' Mostly we have to stop and think about the parts that give us clues. Putting these parts together in our minds can help a reader figure out what the author wants us to think about or feel."

PROJECT: *(Narrative/Informational)* Find *x* number of places in the next two/three/however many chapters where you think the author is giving clues about what she wants you to think about or feel. Jot down a sentence about each. When you are finished, look back over these parts and write a couple of lines about how they do or don't connect.

More Difficult Variation

Teaching Point: "Sometimes authors want us to feel or think about things that don't seem to go together. For example, a story might make us feel sad and hopeful at the same time. Or a nonfiction piece about World War II might make us think about how awful war is, but at the same time how important the issues were that people were

fighting over. In order to understand complicated texts like these, readers need to stop and identify these seeming contradictions and decide what they think about them—or at least consider the questions they raise in our minds."

PROJECT: (*Narrative/Informational*) Find *x* number of places in the next two/three/however many chapters where ideas come up that don't seem to go together. (You might mark them with two different-colored sticky notes or write about them in your reading notebook with different-colored pens.) Look across these parts and write a few lines about why they seem to contradict and what you think the author was trying to say.

Paying Attention to How Things Develop: Tracking Change or the Development of an Idea

Elementary and middle school readers are famous for coming up with one idea and sticking to it, come hell or high water. If the boy is mean at the beginning of the book, even if the whole point of the story is that he secretly has a heart of gold, at the end he remains mean. If the author begins an opinion piece with one point of view and proceeds to raise questions about it, the first argument still holds. This is developmental, in part; if we think back to Piaget, kids at this age are still largely concrete thinkers. We need to teach children that while coming up with an idea in the first place is important, readers must allow their thinking to grow and change as they move through a text. This is not easy for students who are just learning to be flexible in their thinking.

The object of a "Paying Attention to How Things Develop" conference is to provide a scaffold; we want to give young readers specific work to do to practice tracking an idea as it progresses and grows throughout a text.

Easier and More Difficult Variations

(*Narrative/Informational*) *See conference transcript "Mood Thermometer," in Chapter 5.*

Compare and Contrast: Noticing What Is Similar and Different

One of the more accessible entry points for deeper thinking about a text is to compare things—the personalities of two different characters in a story, books by the same author, information about sharks in one book to shark facts from another book. The purpose of a "Compare and Contrast" conference is to help students practice critical thinking within, and eventually across, texts.

Easier Variation

Teaching Point: "One way to think about what you read is to compare things—to think about how they are the same or different. For example, the way two different characters in a story react to something that happens, or Peter's relationship with Fudge compared to his relationship with Sheila. Coming up with ideas about what is the same or different can help readers understand more deeply."

PROJECT: (*Narrative*) Compare two characters' personalities by marking places in the text that show what they are like. (*One way to make this easier to sort is with different-colored sticky notes, e.g., yellow for Ramona and blue for Beezus.*) Write a few lines summarizing what these examples show about each character and how they are the same or different.

More Difficult Variation

Teaching Point: "One way readers get good at understanding books is by comparing them. For example, we might think about how a particular mystery story is or isn't like *most* mysteries, or consider similarities across different Jerry Spinelli books. In informational texts, we may compare the angle, or perspective, of different books about the same historical event. Noticing patterns and differences can help readers understand new, unfamiliar texts by thinking about how they are the same or different from books we already know."

Project: (*Narrative*) Mark places in your mystery/realistic fiction/dystopian novel that seem characteristic (i.e., the sorts of things that happen in other books of the same genre). Also, mark places where this particular book differs. You might want to use one color sticky note for places that seem similar and another color for those that are different. (Or, similarly, mark places in this Jerry Spinelli book that are or aren't like other Jerry Spinelli books.) At the end, write a few lines about what you noticed.

Project: (*Informational*) Mark places in the text where the facts seem to confirm, contradict, or raise questions about information you have read in other books on the same subject. Again, it can be helpful to use different-colored sticky notes or markers to code different types of information.

Reading Like a Writer: Thinking About How the Author Wrote It

"When you read like a reader," says Frank Smith (1983), "you identify with the characters in the story. The story is what you learn about. When you read like a writer, you identify with the author and learn about writing."

While learning about writing is certainly no small thing, I'd argue that Smith's assertion is only part of the puzzle. Thinking about the way an author puts a piece together also gives us greater insight into its meaning. When Malcolm Gladwell begins an article about effective classroom teaching by discussing college football, the reader can't help but marvel at the way he links seemingly unrelated disciplines—and as a result, we see connections that might not have been obvious otherwise. Similarly, when Natalie Babbitt starts *Tuck Everlasting* with a long, poetic setting description, we stop to think about why—and examining her language right off the bat makes us more aware of the imagery that comes later in the book, as the story begins to unfold.

On the other hand, reading and writing are inarguably two sides of the same coin. When students notice craft and structure in books, they read like insiders. In the same way that a trained saxophonist hears different things in a Charlie Parker solo than a non-musician, children begin to think more deeply about texts when they learn to read like writers.

Easier Variation

Teaching Point: "One way readers can get deeply into a book is by paying attention to the language an author uses. When we stop to think about the way an author describes things, and notice the sorts of words they choose to make us see things and feel things, we begin to read with more understanding."

PROJECT: (*Narrative/Informational*) Keep track of places where the author writes a description that really sticks in your mind. Mark it with a sticky note, or copy it into your reading notebook. Write a few words about what you like about it and/or how it helped you understand what was happening in the book more clearly.

More Difficult Variation

This conference is as much metacognitive (i.e., thinking about your thinking) as it is text-based. It is important to remember that these two categories often overlap when we are actually reading. Thinking about them separately is a way to stay focused as teachers, but it should not keep us from showing our students how the two can connect.

Teaching Point: "Sometimes when we come to a confusing part in a book, it is because we missed something, or don't get the language, or too many things are going on at once. But sometimes an author actually *wants* the reader to be confused, so she will keep reading and try to put the pieces together. It's important for us to know the difference between being confused because of something we are not understanding and being confused because the author *wants* us to be (temporarily) confused in that moment."

PROJECT: (*Narrative/Informational*) Keep track of important places in your book where it seems the author *wants* you to be confused. For each one, jot a few words about why you think he/she is purposely doing this. (*Optional:* In addition to marking places the author wants you to be confused, note parts later in the book where the confusion is explained. Jot a few sentences about how and why you think the author did this.)

Go-to Conferences

DEVELOPING A REPERTOIRE

I'm just preparing my impromptu remarks.
—Winston Churchill

Chess, Jazz, and Reading

Professional chess players compete. They need to be acutely aware of each move in the game, not only in the moment, but also to anticipate what may happen next. Since every match is different, chess players must pay attention to what is going on here and now, while keeping in mind strategies that worked in the past. They can't follow scripts. "I missed the strongest move . . ." Grandmaster Garry Kasparov reflected after a rare loss. "I was so entranced by my vision of the gold at the end of this rainbow that I stopped looking around as I approached it."

Jazz musicians improvise. They need to be sensitive to what the band is doing behind them, to the mood in the room—not to mention the structure, harmony, and feeling of the song. Since each performance is a bit different, jazz soloists must be listening and reacting all the time. The best ones never play a song exactly the same way twice. "I can't stand to sing the same song the same way two nights in a row," Billie Holiday famously claimed. "If you can, then it ain't music, it's close order drill, or exercise or yodeling or something, not music."

Clearly, the magical moments in any field are the ones where we invent things we never thought of before—and they turn out to be exactly right.

But no one can count on this happening all the time.

Chess players may not follow scripts, but they do remember past situations. They mix and match strategies encountered before in order to decide how to move forward in each new game. "Chess masters are known for their remarkable memory for the pieces on a chessboard. But it's not because people with photographic memories become chess masters," explains Steven Pinker. "The masters are no better than beginners when remembering a board of randomly arranged pieces. Their memory captures meaningful relations among the pieces, such as threats and defenses, not just their distribution in space." In other words, there are certain setups that occur in many games. The key to being "spontaneous" in chess is knowing which past scenarios may apply to a new situation, and when to apply them.

Similarly, while a jazz musician strives to play something unique in every solo, most have set melodic phrases, or "crips," to draw on as a starting point. Often it is not the actual melodies that are new, but the way they are put together. "I've found," remarked master saxophonist John Coltrane, "that you've got to look back at the old things and see them in a new light." When horn players encounter a predictable song structure—a slow blues or a bright, up-tempo AABA swing tune—they mix and match what they already know to create something original.

It is not so different in the teaching of reading. Developing conference-based reading projects involves listening carefully to what students say about a text, and helping them name an idea worth following. On the surface, it would seem this is not something a teacher can plan for—after all, each child is unique. Moreover, students in a given class may be reading different texts.

The truth is that although no two children are exactly alike, we can often predict directions that a conference with a particular age reader may go. Fourth-grade teachers notice patterns in the sorts of things their nine-year-olds think about as they read; a sixth-grade teacher, like it or not, begins to anticipate the comments of her eleven-year-olds. Some of these conference types have to do with the developmental level, and some are specific to a particular group of students.

Putting knowledge of an age group together with end-year-end expectations for each grade, it is possible to go into a conference with some idea of possible directions—and be ready to mix and match them, when appropriate, for the individual child. Like a jazz soloist or professional chess player, over time a reading teacher may develop a repertoire of "go-to" conferences—or "crips"—to fall back on when a brand new idea is not forthcoming.

Go-to Conferences

The following conferences are gathered from several teachers and schools, all acknowledged along the way. Included are transcripts, with comments interspersed throughout, explaining the teaching moves, sample teaching points and projects in kid-friendly language, possible next steps for future conferences, and easier and more difficult variations. Pay careful attention to the way the words of the students become the basis of the teaching as the teacher names the strategies each young reader is beginning to use, however tentatively. More often than not, it's that thing the child is just a step away from being able to do independently—think Vygotsky's zone of proximal development—which provides us with the best teaching point.

A disclaimer. These transcripts are *not* intended as scripts, but rather as ideas that may or may not be appropriate for an individual child—*depending on what she or he says or does during the conference.* Again, the fundamental tenet of a conference-based reading project is that the direction should come from the student. The idea is that these examples—think of them as *template* conferences—can be a first step in building a storehouse of "go-to" teaching points and projects for a teacher to adapt to the specific thinking of an actual child in his or her class.

Ten Sample Reading Conferences and Possible Projects

Window Parts (Narrative or Informational): Two Prioritizing Conferences

Teaching Point: "It sounds as if you are picturing certain parts in your mind, like looking at them through a window. Readers need to stop when they come to these **window parts**, pay attention to what they are visualizing—and think about why it is important."

We may consider this type of conference when a student

- *gives visual or sensory detail* as she describes a text
- speaks about *how the author wrote it*, e.g., word choice, vivid descriptions, etc.
- *is able to retell, but has a difficult time talking about ideas in books*
- is *trying a new type of text*, i.e., narrative to informational, nonfiction to fiction
- *refers primarily to illustrations and photographs* when discussing a text.

Rationale

Visualizing as we read is not just about picturing beautiful flowers on a hillside. Not that there is anything wrong with having an aesthetic experience in a text; conjuring a beautiful image can certainly help us experience what we read more fully. But picturing something can also be a more analytic thing. Scientists envision theorems as they read complicated papers; mathematicians picture arrays and equations (Keene 2007). Visualizing is a comprehension strategy that serves many purposes and crosses all genres of text. It is a way of solidifying understanding. Ironically though, this most fundamental of comprehension strategies is sometimes poo-pooed in upper grades as unsophisticated. The truth is, readers of all ability levels must learn when and where to visualize.

A Window Parts conference may be sophisticated or simple and can have many points of entry. For example, it could come from a student comment about prioritizing, identifying which parts are important to stop and think about; or it might be appropriate when looking at author's craft, e.g., word choice, where the writer places emphasis.

The two examples that follow illustrate contrasting approaches to working with this strategy.

Cate's Conference (Fourth Grade):

Cate is a fourth grader at Midtown West School who loves to read but is a girl of few words when it comes to talking about her books. Partial to fiction, she strongly identifies with characters; most of her written responses have had to do with feelings and relationships. At the time of this conference, she was making an effort to broaden her reading diet by

tackling a biography of George Washington. According to her teacher Yolen Medard, "Cate is one of my strongest readers, but a goal for her is to think about more than *just* character."

> **Yolen:** *Wow—a historical biography. This is a much different type of book than what you usually read. Tell me about that.*
> **Cate:** *I wanted to try some nonfiction.*
> **Yolen:** *Good for you. So what are you thinking about it?*
> **Cate:** *It's different.*
> **Yolen:** *How does it feel different to read nonfiction? Do you have to do different things to understand?*

Most teachers will recognize this sort of scenario. Cate has not volunteered much information, and it would be easy to feel at a loss for a direction. How can we base the conference on the kid's thinking when there is so little to go on? Yolen's last question, though, takes the conversation in another direction. By asking Cate what she does in her head to read nonfiction, she has positioned herself as one reader talking to another, genuinely wanting to share strategies. Very different than a teacher looking for an answer which may or may not be the right one.

Cate: Well, it does feel different. In fiction, I feel like I'm IN it, like I'm part of the book.

Yolen: Say more about that.

Cate: Well, I feel the same things the character is feeling. It's like I'm there in the book, I'm in that world and not the real world.

Yolen: So in nonfiction you don't feel that way?

Cate: No. With nonfiction it's like I'm seeing it in my mind. I'm more conscious of my surroundings. It's like I'm looking at it through a little window or something.

It's worth noticing that Yolen has not yet asked about the specific book Cate is reading, but rather about her habits as a reader. Moreover, when the student explains what it's like for her to read fiction ("I'm in that world and not the real world"), Yolen harks back to her earlier comment that nonfiction is different and pushes Cate to explain the contrast. Sometimes asking students to explain how something is different provides a jumping-off point for deepening their thinking.

In these few exchanges, Cate and Yolen have co-constructed a lens for looking at nonfiction—arguably a more useful direction than enumerating facts about George Washington. Rather than abandoning this more general idea to talk about the specifics of the book, Yolen now names—and frames—what her student is doing as a teaching point, something to keep in mind for future reading. She also suggests making it the basis of Cate's conference-based reading project.

Yolen: That is so interesting. One thing that is really important for readers to do is stop and pay attention to places where they get those clear pictures in their mind—those window parts—and think about how they go together. Would you like to do some work like that with this George Washington book?

Cate: You mean mark the parts where I see it in my mind?

Yolen: Yes. And then maybe look them over and think about which ones go together.

Cate: That sounds cool. I can write about that in my reading notebook. (See Figures 5.1a and 5.1b.)

The Next Conference Could Be . . .

Teaching Point: "Some of what readers envision when they encounter window parts is described in the text itself—but they also add information of their own. It is important to pay attention to which parts of the 'movie in your mind' come from the actual words on the page and which we imagine for other reasons."

PROJECT: Make a two-column chart of what you picture that's *not* in the words and what makes you picture it.

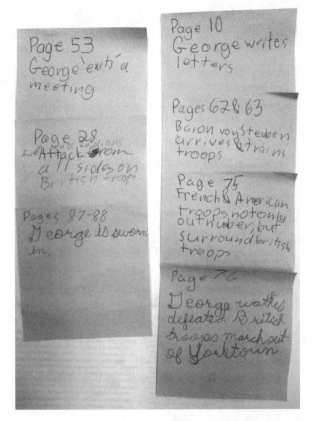

Figure 5.1a Cate's George Washington "Window Parts" Sticky Notes

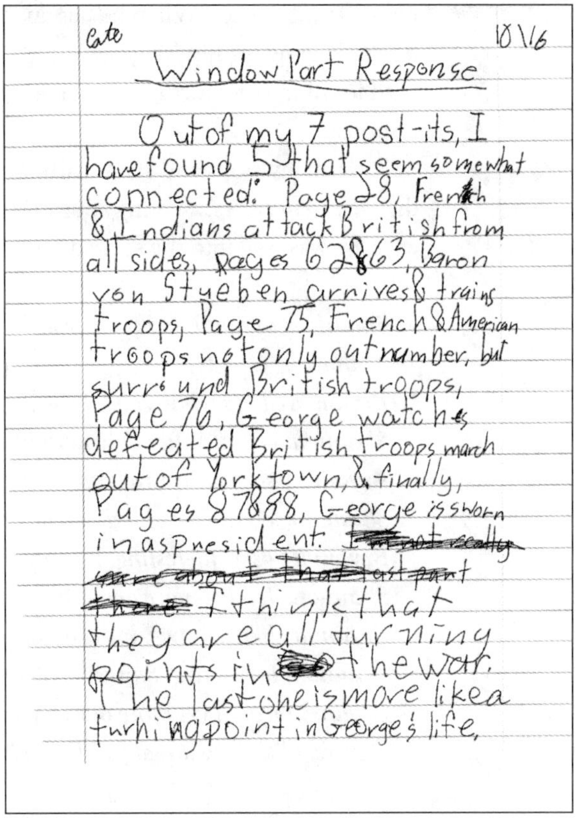

Figure 5.1b Cate's final response. Reflecting on the parts where she was moved to visualize, she writes "I think that they are all turning points in the war. The last one was a turning point in George's life."

Teaching Point: "Readers know that a mental picture can be accompanied by an idea, a question, or a strong feeling."

PROJECT: For each window part, record where you have questions/ideas/feelings and code them (e.g., "Q," "I," or "F"). Look across these. Do you tend to do one more than another?

Bryan's Conference (Seventh Grade):

Bryan attends Special Music School, I.S. 859 in New York City, where his enthusiasm for school is sometimes at odds with his academic progress. Although a hard worker, his lower grade on the standardized state test placed him in mandated extended day for the year, which did not help his self-confidence. "When he has an idea," says Shannon Potts, Bryan's English teacher, "it can be challenging for him to get it out. He is a positive kid and will tell you he loves a book, but it's hard for him to get further than that. Often he just sits doodling when it's time to write a reading response."

After many stops and starts with texts that he ultimately abandoned, Bryan finally settled on the *Divergent* series, a young adult trilogy about a dystopian society. At the time of this conference, he was well into the second book, *Insurgent*.

> **Shannon:** *Bryan! It looks like you're powering through* Insurgent. *Tell me what you are thinking about.*
>
> **Bryan:** *Well, it's really good. Like, it's really good.*
>
> **Shannon:** *Great! What do you think makes it really good?*
>
> **Bryan:** *It's so good I stayed up until eleven last night reading it.*
>
> **Shannon:** *What makes it different from the other books you've read?*
>
> **Bryan:** *It's very interesting. It really pulls me in.*
>
> **Shannon:** *Tell me more about that.*
>
> **Bryan:** *It's like a movie, but a book.*
>
> **Shannon:** *Interesting. Say more about how it's like a movie.*
>
> **Bryan:** *I mean, I get more out of a book than a movie, but I can really* see *what's going on here. I like how it really pulls me in.*

Shannon: I'm so excited that the book is pulling you in! Can you tell me what's making it so compelling for you?

Bryan: Well, while I'm reading I see a visual at the same time—I see people talking and things happening. That doesn't always happen when I read.

It is interesting to note that Shannon introduces no content of her own for this whole first part of the conference. After initially asking what Bryan is thinking about, every follow-up response is some version of *say more about that*—with the important caveat that she also repeats his language back to him (e.g., "really good," "like a movie," "pulling me in"), signaling that she is actively listening and interested in what he has to say. By the fifth (count 'em) *tell me more*, the student's thinking is much deeper, more specific—something to go on. And Shannon seizes the opportunity.

Shannon: When readers are able to see what is happening in the book in their mind, it means their understanding is pretty deep. In these moments, when you come on those "movie type" parts, it could be interesting work for you to stop and explore that picture in your head. What are you seeing, and why does it pull you in?

Bryan: Maybe I could draw it.

Shannon: That would be fabulous. How about drawing what you see at that key moment when you are pulled in, and saying why it got you interested?

Bryan: Really? I can do that?

Here was the moment of truth. By allowing Bryan to leverage his strength—he is, after all, a doodler—Shannon engaged him in some significant comprehension work. The work he produced was quite impressive, and showed a real ability to infer detail. Some of the moments he ended up sketching were not literal images described in the book, but they fit perfectly in context (see Figures 5.2a and 5.2b). "From here, Bryan got a lot bolder with expressing his own opinions about what he was reading," Shannon commented. "It's like making the drawings, and then talking off of them, opened him up."

The Next Conference Could Be . . .

Teaching Point: "Readers know to pay special attention to the window parts in a book that help them visualize, or see the scene in their minds. There are other parts that draw us into the text by creating a strong feeling (e.g., sad, angry, happy). These are also important to stop and think about."

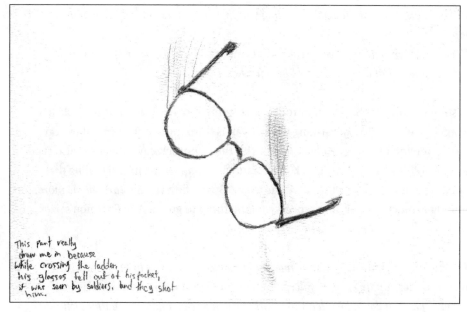

This part really drew me in because while crossing the ladder, his glasses fell out of his pocket, it was seen by soldiers, and they shot him.

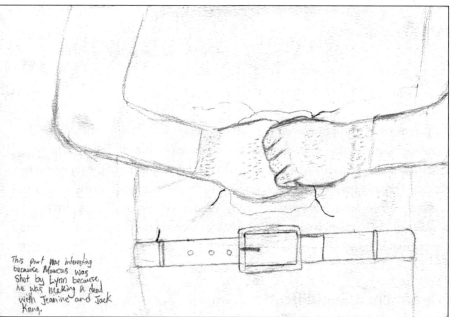

This part was interesting because Marcus was shot by Lynn because he was making a deal with Jeanine and Jack Kang.

Figures 5.2a and 5.2b Some sketches from Bryan's *Insurgent* project. In the first one, we see him isolating the visual image that triggered the important action ("his glasses fell out of his pocket, it was seen by soldiers, and they shot him"). In the second, he imagines a character's hands clenched tightly over a wound—not an image described in the book. "He was inferring more than I'd thought," commented Shannon.

Project 1: Find one strong feeling part in each chapter. Jot down how it makes you feel and why.

Project 2: Connect strong feeling parts to window parts. Do any of the places that make you visualize also give you strong feelings?

More Difficult Variation

Teaching Point: "Window parts are often places an author wants us to pay attention, but they do not always stand alone; often, there are other important passages that connect to the visual scene. For example, if we have read about a character's feeling elsewhere in the text, we might picture a particular facial expression. As readers stop and picture a scene, they need to think about other passages in the text that connect and help them visualize."

Project: For each window part, find one other passage elsewhere in the text that connects in some way. Explain the connection.

Detail Addition (Narrative/Informational): Two Connecting the Dots Conferences

Teaching Point: "Sometimes reading is like an addition problem in math. You put one detail together with another, and then another, and then you come up with an idea. Detail + detail + detail = an idea. We could call it **detail addition**."

We may consider this type of conference when a student

- can give a basic retell but has a hard time discussing smaller details and why they may be important
- *lists lots of details in describing her thoughts about a book without connecting them*, e.g., character traits in a narrative or which facts are most important in an informational text
- *makes a judgment about something in the text but does not give specific evidence*. This could be a generalization about a character's motivation ("She was probably jealous," "He was trying to teach them a lesson"), what the theme might be ("I think it's

about sticking up for your friends"), or simply summing up an observation about a chunk of text ("Back then, kids had different jobs to do than today," "She was the quiet one in the family"). The important thing is that it is an idea based on several details put together.

Rationale

As with most things in life, learning to synthesize starts small. Children in earlier grades first need to practice connecting parts of a single chapter, different sections of an article, or sometimes even sentences on the same page. By upper elementary school, however, deciding which passages connect often requires thinking across multiple pages. A Detail Addition conference allows for simple or more complicated variations.

What follows are two versions of a Detail Addition conference: a third grader reading a Laura Ingalls Wilder novel, and a fifth-grade student working with an informational text about animals.

Henry's Conference (Narrative, Third Grade):

Henry is a student at Midtown West Elementary School who understands the broad strokes of a story, but seldom has much to say beyond a basic retell. "He's a pretty strong reader when it comes to just telling what happened," explains third-grade teacher Kay Loua. "But his attention to detail isn't great, so in the end he misses a lot. I'm worried this is going to catch up with him when the books get harder."

Going in to the conference, Kay and I wanted to listen for something Henry might say that could lead to work around identifying important details—but the entry point had to come from him.

> **Dan:** *So Henry, you are reading* Farmer Boy *by Laura Ingalls Wilder. What are you think-ing about this book?*
> **Henry:** *Well, I read the first one,* Little House on the Prairie, *too. I like this one better.*
> **Dan:** *Say more about that.*
> **Henry:** *This one has more stuff about animals. I like animals.*
> **Dan:** *So the animal stuff is making it interesting? I'd love to hear more about that.*

At this point, Henry began to retell the plot of *Farmer Boy*, with no particular reference to why the animals were important. Predictably, when asked to go a bit deeper, he fell back on what he knew—telling what happened in the story. At moments like these, a teacher needs to gently nudge the student back on track. So as not to take away ownership of the conference, it is important to resist the temptation to leap in too quickly with an agenda, but instead go back to something *the student* said earlier.

> **Dan:** *Thanks for telling me the story. I'd like to go back to what you said earlier, about the animal stuff. Can you show me a part in the book about animals that was interesting to you?*
>
> **Henry:** *(Searches through the book, at first randomly—then he remembers a particular chapter and flips to it.) Right here. This part shows Almanzo with the animals. He's working with the cows.*
>
> **Dan:** *Working with them?*
>
> **Henry:** *Yeah, he's sort of teaching the younger cows how to be older cows.*
>
> **Dan:** *Interesting. Say more about that.*
>
> **Henry:** *Well, for example, he's showing them how to go left and then right. Also, he's teaching them how to go giddy-up, to go faster. And how to stop when they are supposed to.*

Here was the moment. Henry had shown not only an awareness of details but had connected them, albeit with a bit of nudging. Although a fairly literal inference, "teaching them to be older cows" shows a beginning ability to interpret beyond the text. And the thinking work was his, not the teacher's. At this point, it is important to step in and *name* the strategy for the student so it can become internalized.

> **Dan:** *Wow, Henry. Look at what you just did. Laura Ingalls Wilder doesn't say anywhere in this book that Almanzo was teaching them to be older cows. But* you *put together a bunch of details to figure that out. Showing them how to go left and right, PLUS teaching them how to giddy-up, PLUS teaching them to stop, EQUALS teaching them to be older cows. Do you see how you put together those details to come up with your own idea?*
>
> **Henry:** *Yes, well when you add them up that's really what he is doing.*
>
> **Dan:** *I agree. And you came up with your* own *words to describe it that the author didn't even say.*

Having gone over the specific example in the book, the teacher then needs to state the teaching point in a way that could apply to the next book, and the book after that.

> **Dan:** *One thing that is really important for readers to always do is add up details to come up with their own idea.* **It's a little like an addition problem in math. This detail, plus that detail, plus that other detail, equals my idea.** *Do you think there might be*

other places in the book where you are putting together details to come up with your own idea?

Henry agreed that keeping track of places where he adds up details to come up with his own idea would make for an interesting reading project. Together, we negotiated that he would find three other examples over the next two chapters and set them up like math problems. In addition, he'd jot down a few lines about how it felt to do this work (see Figure 5.3).

Figure 5.3 Henry's "Detail Addition" work. While his connections are fairly literal, the word choice ("sugar snow," "teaching the cows how to grow up") shows that Henry is beginning to interpret what he reads in his own way.

Now that the logistics had been ironed out, it was important to end with a connection to future reading.

> **Dan:** *This is pretty exciting, Henry. I think this project is going to help you practice thinking about which details connect, and how they can add up to something bigger. As books get harder, there are always more details to keep track of. So practicing this is going to help you read even more difficult books.*

The example conference above is of moderate difficulty, dealing with concrete details (i.e., character's actions), and ending with a sort of summing up ("He's teaching them to be older cows"). Again, it's a pretty literal inference, though Henry's choice of words does show some ability to interpret events in his own way; after all, he *could* have just said Almanzo was *training* the cows. The work he turned in later continued along this same line, and all of his examples involved connecting details within the same chapter.

The Next Conference Could Be . . .

Teaching Point: "Sometimes readers connect details to understand what is happening in the text, and sometimes they connect details to come up with their own opinion."

Project 1: Put three or more details together across chapters to come up with an idea about a character's personality, or a relationship between two characters.

Project 2: Add three or more details across chapters to come up with an idea about the setting.

Project 3: Add three or more details to come up with an opinion about what a character should do, or what the author should have happen next.

Easier Variation

Teaching Point: "Readers connect details from different parts of the same page in order to understand what they read."

Project: Connect two details on the same page, and say what they tell the reader about what the character is doing/what the character's personality is like/how the character is feeling.

More Difficult Variations

Teaching Point: "Readers connect details to better understand the author's point of view and what she or he wants us to think about or feel."

Project: Add up three (or four, or six) details across chapters that suggest what the author *wants readers to think about*, or *feel*, as they read the story (theme).

Teaching Point: "Sometimes the key to understanding a text is to think about details that *seem to contradict each other* and consider how they do or don't go together."

Project: Find *x* examples of details that *seem to contradict each other* about character relationships or theme, and set up a detail addition problem that explains what you think the author is trying to say.

Katerina's Conference (Informational, Fifth Grade):

Katerina, who we met as a fourth grader in Chapter 1, is now an avid fifth-grade reader who usually gravitates to fiction when left to her own devices. Her class was beginning a nonfiction unit at the time of this conference. "Katerina likes animal books in her fiction reading," explains Hallie Saltz, her teacher at Manhattan New School, "so I wasn't surprised when she chose *Cats vs. Dogs*, from a National Geographic series."

> *Dan: Cats versus dogs, eh? Sounds like a battle or something.*
> *Katerina: Well, no, not exactly. It's just about who is better at doing what, like cleaning themselves or hearing small movements.*
> *Dan: Hmm, interesting examples. Can you say more about that?*
> *Katerina: (flipping the pages) The way the pages are, it like goes back and forth between dogs and cats, and says who it is and why.*
> *Dan: Interesting. So the author uses a particular structure. What do you think about that?*

Here Katerina has volunteered specific examples in describing her book, showing a good ability to pick out what is important. When asked to say more, her next move is to look at the alternating structure of the book, rather than retelling facts. Since she had moved on to thinking about the bigger picture, i.e., the purpose of the text, it made sense to ask about *her* thinking. Katerina rose to the challenge.

> *Katerina: I think you are supposed to compare them and notice what is the same and what's different.*

Dan: *Can you tell me about a place where you compared two facts?*

Katerina: *Right here it talks about how cats have very strong hearing, and they run away when there are loud sounds. But dogs tuck their ears and hunch their backs to appear smaller.*

Dan: *So what does that make you think?*

Katerina: *I guess it shows that cats and dogs have very different ways to express their feelings.*

Bingo. Katerina had not only connected two facts, but had actually made a judgment—an inference—by putting them together. It was time to pull back and name what she did in a way that went beyond *Cats vs. Dogs* and could be generalized to other information books.

Dan: *You know what I just heard you doing, Katerina? You put together two facts and came up with your own idea. Nonfiction always has a lot of facts, and one of the big challenges for a reader is figuring out ways to keep track of them. One way is to connect facts, like you just did, and decide what you think about them once they are put together. You can think of it like a math problem:* this fact + that fact = my idea. *For example,* cats have very strong hearing and run away + dogs hunch their backs = cats and dogs have different ways to express their feelings. *It's like fact addition.*

Katerina: *Cool. I guess I did do that!*

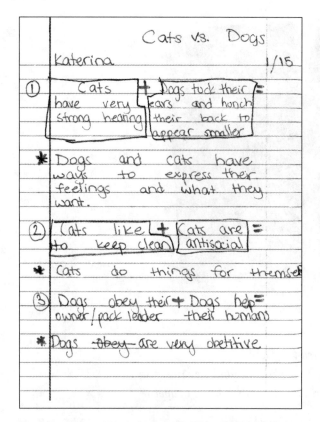

Figures 5.4a and 5.4b Katerina's "Fact Addition" work from the book *Cats vs. Dogs*. The facts she was adding together are numbered, with her idea, or inference, below, next to the asterisk.

> **Dan:** *How would you like to do a reading project where you practice adding facts together to come up with your own idea as you continue with* Cats vs. Dogs? *(See Figures 5.4a and 5.4b.)*

It is rare for a student to hand a teacher a conference direction on a platter. More often, we need to listen to what the student says and observe what she does, then name it. Katerina demonstrated an ability not just to connect two facts, but also to make a larger inference beyond the literal once she had put them together (i.e., "cats and dogs have very different ways to express their feelings"). Here is an example of a conference where the teaching point and project came from naming what a student did, rather than extending something she said.

Asking "Why?" at Surprising Parts (Narrative): Thinking About Your Thinking Conference

Teaching Point: "Readers can't pay equal attention to every single thing that happens in a story. Parts where something surprising happens are usually important. When these parts come up, readers need to stop and ask, '*Why* did this happen?' Answering that question helps us understand the story better as it continues to develop."

We may consider this type of conference when a student

- mostly retells but is *beginning to express opinions within the retell*
- comments on *reasons a character said or did something* in the story
- notices how *actions and feelings connect* in a text.

Rationale

One way to look at reading is as a series of choices. A reader must make decisions along the way about which things in the text are most important and where to stop and pay special attention. It is helpful for students to see teachers demonstrate this stopping and thinking, in order to learn some of the habits of mind involved in deciding what is important. But simply prioritizing is not enough; along the way, children also need to learn *what readers do in their heads* when they stop to think about a particular passage.

Moments in stories where unexpected things happen are always good places to stop and think. Often these parts are surprising because we've been led to believe the plot is going another way, and now we must reset our expectations. Before reading on, it is helpful to think about what, exactly, led up to the unexpected event. Teaching children the simple strategy of asking "Why?" at such moments is one way to take control and not be passive at moments of confusion.

Abigail's Conference (Fourth Grade):

Abigail is a grade-level reader who asks a variety of questions, both in her independent books and during whole-class read-alouds. Some of these are higher level, and some are of the basic clear-up-plot-confusion type. "She tends to think a lot about character," says teacher Jamie Kushner, "but isn't quite thinking about theme yet, at least independently. She's much better at talking about what's in the book than what's going on in her head. I think getting more metacognitive might be the next step in pushing Abigail to think more deeply."

At the time of this conference, Abigail was a few chapters in to *These Happy Golden Years*, a book in Laura Ingalls Wilder's Little House series.

Jamie: So Abigail, I see you are reading more historical fiction. What are you thinking about this book?

Abigail: Well, there's this character named Mrs. Brewster and she's really mean. Actually the whole family is mean, and this girl Laura has to live with them.

Jamie: So Mrs. Brewster is mean. Can you say more about that?

Abigail: The way she treats her son. It's like she doesn't want him to have fun. I don't know why a mother would do that to her own son.

Jamie: It sounds like you find that surprising.

Abigail: Yes.

Jamie: So you are wondering why. Do you have any ideas?

Abigail: (shrugs) I'm not sure. Maybe she's taking her own anger out on her son.

Jamie: Can you say more about that?

Abigail: (after several seconds of silence) I'm not sure. Laura just came to live with them. Maybe she doesn't like Laura and doesn't want her to think she is nice.

A lot has happened in these first few exchanges. For starters, not surprisingly, Abigail begins with a retell. Jamie, undaunted, listens for some idea, any idea, and finds it in the comment that Mrs. Brewster is "really mean." Not rocket science, but an opinion nonetheless, and so she asks her student to say more. Abigail responds with a good example, but Jamie doesn't stop there. Instead she asks Abigail to elaborate ("It sounds like you find that surprising. . . . Do you have any ideas about that?"). Now Abigail becomes more thoughtful, and knowing that several "Say more about that" comments often result in deeper thinking, Jamie pushes for still more.

Interestingly, after some wait time, rather than continuing with the idea that Mrs. Brewster is "taking her own anger out," the student comes back with another possibility. The temptation here might be to not let Abigail off the hook, to push her to say more about her original thought. Instead, Jamie chooses to name what her young reader has done well so far.

Jamie: Abigail, you have done a couple of really interesting things here. For one, you stopped and thought about a part that was surprising, not what you would have expected—a mother being mean to her son. Then you asked why. *I am wondering, are you usually the kind of reader who stops at surprising parts and asks* why?

Abigail: I guess I am.

Jamie: Readers of stories need to know where to stop and think. One important place to pay attention is at a surprising part. If you just keep going when something unexpected happens, you may get confused. But if you stop and ask *why,* you can often understand even better. Would you agree?

Abigail: Yes.

Jamie: But you did something else. You didn't stop with just one answer, you came up with two—*taking out her own anger,* and *showing Laura she wasn't nice. Can you say more about that?*

Abigail: Well, it seemed like it could have been either. I have to see what happens later.

Jamie: I think you are on to something here. When you come up with two ideas instead of one, there's more to think about. And the more you think, the more you understand.

Abigail: That's true.

Jamie: How would you like to do a reading project where you practice asking *why* at surprising parts, and coming up with two possible answers?

Abigail: That'd be interesting.

Here is a clear example of a teaching point coming out of naming what a student has done. It's significant to note, though, that none of Jamie's comments "led the witness"—without exception, everything she asked was a direct response to something Abigail said or did. At several points, she positioned her student as a reader capable of reflecting on her own thinking (i.e., ". . . are you usually the kind of reader who stops at surprising parts and asks *why*?" "Would you agree?"), and Abigail rose to the challenge (see Figures 5.5a and 5.5b).

The Next Conference Could Be . . .

Teaching Point: "Now that we've practiced asking 'Why?' at surprising parts, it could be interesting to go one step further and think about the author's choices. Why did she choose to put in a surprising part at that moment? How did it make the story more interesting? What sorts of questions did she want to put in the reader's mind? Thinking about what the author is doing not only helps us understand the story better, but it can also teach us things to use in our own writing."

PROJECT: Find one surprising part in each of the next three (or more!) chapters. In your notebook, mark the page number and write what you think the author was trying to do in this surprising part; for example, put questions in the reader's mind, shock the reader, making the story more interesting in the following way, mislead the reader, etc. (depending on what the student says during the conference!).

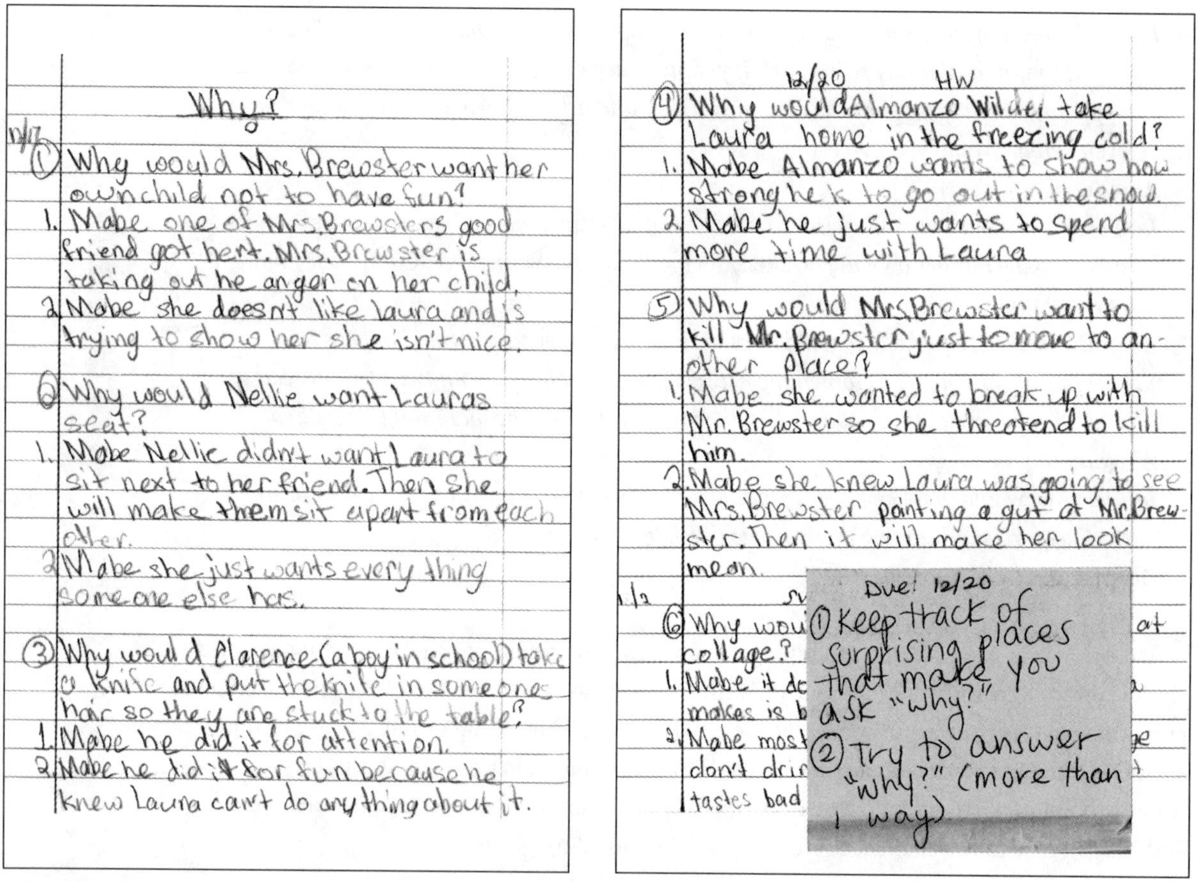

Why?

11/17

① Why would Mrs. Brewster want her own child not to have fun?
1. Mabe one of Mrs. Brewsters good friend got hert. Mrs. Brewster is taking out her anger on her child.
2. Mabe she doesn't like Laura and is trying to show her she isn't nice.

② Why would Nellie want Lauras seat?
1. Mabe Nellie didn't want Laura to sit next to her friend. Then she will make them sit apart from each other.
2. Mabe she just wants every thing some one else has.

③ Why would Clarence (a boy in school) take a knife and put the knife in someone hair so they are stuck to the table?
1. Mabe he did it for attention.
2. Mabe he did it for fun because he knew Laura can't do any thing about it.

12/20   HW
④ Why would Almanzo Wilder take Laura home in the freezing cold?
1. Mabe Almanzo wants to show how strong he is to go out in the snow.
2. Mabe he just wants to spend more time with Laura

⑤ Why would Mrs. Brewster want to kill Mr. Brewster just to move to another place?
1. Mabe she wanted to break up with Mr. Brewster so she threatend to kill him.
2. Mabe she knew Laura was going to see Mrs. Brewster painting a gut at Mr. Brewster. Then it will make her look mean.

⑥ Why wou... collage?
1. Mabe it de... makes is b...
2. Mabe most... don't dri... tastes bad

Due! 12/20
① Keep track of surprising places that make you ask "why?"
② Try to answer "why?" (more than 1 way)

Figures 5.5a and 5.5b Abigail's list of surprising parts, written in the form of "Why?" questions. Notice Jamie's sticky note at the bottom. Many teachers choose to leave the student with a reminder at the end of each conference.

Easier Variation

Teaching Point: "Authors of stories often try to surprise the reader. In order to understand the story well, we need to decide when a surprising part is important enough to stop and think about, and when it may *not* be so important."

PROJECT: As you read, put sticky notes on the surprising parts. Every few chapters, stop and think about which ones are important and which ones are not so important. Organize them into two groups in your notebook, and write a few sentences about what you've noticed.

Grouping Facts (Informational Text): Connecting the Dots/Prioritizing Conference

Teaching Point: "Information books have way too many facts for anyone to remember them all. Readers of nonfiction need to develop strategies to keep track of information that is important. One way to do this is to **connect facts that seem to go together**."

We may consider this type of conference when a student

- is beginning to *refer back to earlier parts of the book when retelling* interesting facts
- is *learning to prioritize facts* in her nonfiction reading
- has begun *learning note-taking skills*.

Rationale

One of the biggest hurdles children face when learning to read informational text is figuring out what to prioritize. Although determining importance is a critical comprehension strategy unto itself, once students begin to separate out important facts from not-so-important ones, they must also learn how to organize and group the information. In truth, these skills are not so separate; sometimes making connections between related information tells us *what* to prioritize.

A common mistake is to leap straight to note-taking skills before teaching students how to organize important information in their heads. A Grouping Facts conference can be just the interim step to address this need.

Dyandra's Conference (Third Grade):

Dyandra is a student at PS 369 in the South Bronx, one of the poorest congressional districts in the country. Although a diligent student, she is reading significantly below grade level. Dyandra has mastered the skill of retelling, but has great difficulty discussing what she thinks about what she is reading. At the time of this conference, she had just chosen (for the first time!) an informational book for independent reading—a significant departure from her usual realistic fiction about kids in school.

> **Dan:** *So Dyandra, what are you reading?*
> **Dyandra:** *It's a book called* From Flowers to Fruit.
> **Dan:** *Nonfiction! Is that the kind of book you normally like to read?*

> *Dyandra:* Not really.
>
> *Dan:* So what made you choose this one today?
>
> *Dyandra:* (shrugs) I don't know. Maybe because I like to look at flowers.
>
> *Dan:* Ah, so you were interested in this particular subject. Ms. Cruz told me you usually like books that talk about character's feelings. I imagine you have to do different things in your head when you're reading a book like this. Can you say more about that?
>
> *Dyandra:* I pretend that it is another kind of book, not nonfiction.
>
> *Dan:* What kind of stuff has been interesting so far?
>
> *Dyandra:* Well, on this page it has a lot of flowers that this kind of animal likes (points)— this kind of flower—and the bats, too, like different kinds of flowers than the birds. And the hummingbirds, they like this kind of flower.
>
> *Dan:* That is so interesting, Dyandra. You were telling me that you usually like books with characters and feelings, and then you picked a part about which flowers the different animals like. That's kind of telling the animals' feelings, isn't it? And it helped you with nonfiction. So you are really a feelings kind of reader.
>
> *Dyandra:* (smiles) Yup. I guess I really am.

Knowing that Dyandra has difficulty discussing her reading, we went in to the conference prepared to provide more scaffolding than is usual in a project-based reading conference. Nonetheless, the opening questions (i.e., "I imagine you have to do different things in your head when you're reading a book like this") subtly position Dyandra as a person capable of thinking about her thinking. Although her initial response wasn't particularly convincing ("I pretend that it is another kind of book, not nonfiction"), it was a first try—and swooping in to correct or ask for clarification could have been a potentially discouraging move. Instead, we went back to talking about the specifics of the text—a place Dyandra felt more secure—and took the opportunity to point out something about *who she is as a reader* (". . . you are really a feelings kind of reader").

Naming what she does well is not a small thing for a student like Dyandra. One of the many issues for struggling readers is that they do not feel like they are members of the club, and are typically unaware that they even *have* an identity as a reader. Dyandra's positive response left her open to the next challenge.

> *Dan:* The other thing you did that I wanted to ask about is you compared *facts—you said* "Here's a flower that the bird likes, and here's a kind of flower that the bat likes." That's called comparing and contrasting, *saying who likes what and how it's different. Is there any other place in this book where you saw two facts and put them together?*
>
> *Dyandra:* Yeah. (points to diagram) Here, in the flower. This and this are almost the same thing, these two parts—the carpel and the stamen. They do the same thing.

Dan: *Look at what you just did! You compared what the bird likes to what the bat likes, and then you compared the carpel to the stamen. To read information books well, it is so important to do what you are doing right now. And this is a new kind of book for you, so you're just getting started, right?*

Dyandra: *That's right.*

Dan: *The thing about information books is that there are so many facts, it's impossible to remember them all. One way to remember important things, to get really good at reading information books, is to notice which facts connect. And you just connected four facts—the bat to the bird, and the carpel to the stamen!*

Dyandra: *And then you could remember them.*

Dan: *How would you like to do a project where you practice connecting facts?*

Dyandra: *Good idea.*

Our most struggling readers seldom articulate a clear line of thinking about a text. Teachers must harness their "kidwatching" skills (Goodman 2002) and get good at noticing and naming what the child is doing. On the surface, Dyandra's comments could easily have been dismissed as retelling; digging a little deeper, and again, naming exactly *how* she was retelling, lifted the student's thinking—not to mention her confidence—to another level. Now that she was willing to go further with connecting facts, the final step was to negotiate the reading project.

Figure 5.6 Dyandra's reading work. As a lower-level reader, it's interesting to note how some of her sticky notes indicating connecting facts are on the pictures rather than on the text. Allowing Dyandra to refer to both images and words helps scaffold the complex work of synthesizing information for the first time.

Dan: Here's what I'm thinking. Where are you up to in this book?

Dyandra: (points) Right here, page 13.

Dan: Let's go back to the carpel and stamen page. You said this fact goes with this fact, right? (Dyandra nods.) Let's put one sticky note on the stamen part and another one, the same color, on the carpel part. (Dyandra does so.) OK, write a letter A on each of them. (Dyandra does this.) The reason I asked you to do this is because those two facts go together, right? (Dyandra nods.) So now let's find the other two facts that connect.

Dyandra: The ones about the bird and the bat. Should I put stickies on them, too?

Dan: Yup—and this time put B and B since these two go together.

In order for Dyandra to be successful, it was important to help her create a concrete, simple way to do the complex work of organizing facts. In the end, she chose to find five different pairs of connecting facts—and along the way, internalized an important habit of mind that will serve her in future nonfiction reading.

The Next Conference Could Be . . .

Teaching Point: "Once readers of nonfiction begin to connect facts that go together, they often notice *groups of facts* that fall into certain categories. For example, when reading about people of a certain country, they may notice several facts about their religion, and other information about their food. To keep track of this new information, they begin to think of what they are learning by putting it into groups, or *categories*."

Project: Look across the different connecting facts you have marked, and put them into two (or three, or four) groups. Write a few sentences about why they go together, and note if any *don't* fall into a group.

Mood Thermometer (Narrative): Paying Attention to How Things Develop Conference

Teaching Point: "Authors want us to feel different ways at different parts of a story. It's important for us to have a sort of mood thermometer in our heads, where we keep track of how the mood of the book changes."

We may consider this type of conference when a student

- talks about *the mood of a story* (e.g., "It's really sad")
- comments on *the way a character feels*
- notices how *actions and feelings connect*.

Rationale

In the earliest grades, characters in stories tend to be one-dimensional. Particularly in series books for primary ages (e.g., *Nate the Great, George and Martha*), the characters' personalities don't change in significant ways and their moods are pretty predictable. This is, of course, a good thing; it's that very predictability that scaffolds our youngest readers' early efforts to make meaning.

As books get harder though, one of the biggest shifts in the way stories go is that characters often change, or develop, from the beginning to the end. Even when there is no major personality overhaul, at the very least they *feel* different ways at different points throughout the book. It follows then that the reader too is supposed to experience different emotions along the way.

Often when we describe a book, our tendency is to over generalize; it is a sad story, or a happy one, or suspenseful. The truth is, very few texts maintain one feeling all the way through. Usually there are moments we feel sad, but other parts where we feel hopeful, angry, excited, etc.

Readers of narratives must not only keep track of the changing feelings of the characters in the story, but also be aware of how the author wants the *reader* to feel throughout the book. A Mood Thermometer conference can support a student in keeping track of how such feelings evolve as a story develops.

Vanessa's Conference (Fifth Grade):

Vanessa started the school year slightly below grade level. A diligent worker who takes great pride in her reading achievements, she nonetheless reads at a slow pace and says little in class booktalks. When she does discuss her reading, Vanessa has difficulty coming up with evidence to support her thinking and tends to just retell plot events. "During partner talks, she spends a lot of time searching for parts in the book that back up her ideas," says Sophie Brady, her teacher at Manhattan New School. "My goal for Vanessa is to practice identifying supporting details as she reads, to strengthen her arguments."

At the time of this conference, Vanessa was just a few chapters into *Nory Ryan's Song*, a historical fiction novel by Patricia Reilly Giff.

> **Dan:** *So Vanessa, what are you thinking about this book?*
> **Vanessa:** *Well, it's sort of depressing.*
> **Dan:** *How so?*
> **Vanessa:** *Because Nory's sister Maggie is leaving to go to Brooklyn, New York. In Ireland they don't have that much freedom, that's why she's going to Brooklyn, New York. And Nory really wants to go as their whole family, but they can't because they can't afford it.*
> **Dan:** *Interesting. You just told me all these details of the story—but the first thing you said is that it's depressing. Can you say more about which details were depressing?*
> **Vanessa:** *The detail about Maggie leaving was a depressing one.*

Though she does begin the conference by expressing an opinion ("it's sort of depressing"), Vanessa responds to the follow-up question by retreating to her place of safety—telling what happened in the book. Asking her to "say more about which details were depressing" helped link the original idea to the retell, and Vanessa was able to come up with some evidence, however tentatively. The next step was to encourage her to go further.

> **Dan:** *Hmm. You also mentioned the "no freedom in Ireland" thing, that's not very happy, and of course Maggie leaving. So it seems there are a couple of depressing things.*
> **Vanessa:** *(nods) Yeah.*
> **Dan:** *Was there one particular place where you were reading and just said to yourself, "Oh my gosh, this is so depressing"?*
> **Vanessa:** *(Leafs through book for several seconds, then smiles.) It's right here. (Reads aloud) "I wanted to sink down too. Instead I brushed my hands across my hair. I bent over, holding Patch the way Maggie would have, rocking him."*
> **Dan:** *I can see why you chose that part—she's obviously not happy. So what did that make you think?*
> **Vanessa:** *It made me think that Maggie was an important person to Nory. And that was depressing because they were crying, and Nory was trying to do what Maggie would have done. That's depressing because you don't really know what she would do.*

Knowing Vanessa's difficulty in elaborating on her ideas, it seemed appropriate to give her some sort of prompt—but the important thing (always!) is that it comes from *her* thinking. Since she had mentioned the "no freedom in Ireland" thing in the course of her retell, using that as a basis for the next question pushed her to say more without taking away ownership of the idea. It made sense then to bring Vanessa back to the text—solid ground, no searching around in her memory—and ask her to find a part to illustrate her thinking, then and there. She responded with her most articulate comments so far.

The next step was to *name* what Vanessa had done—and call it out as a teaching point.

Dan: *You know, Vanessa, when we read stories, the author wants us to pay attention to what the characters are feeling— but she wants the reader to feel something, too. It's not like it happens all through the book; there are certain places where a light goes off and a feeling comes up. That's what happened for you in this part—you read it and thought "Wow, this book is depressing." Do you imagine it's going to stay depressing the entire book through, or do you think there will be other feelings in there?*

Vanessa: *No. I think there might be more feelings in there. Because there was a part where Nory went fishing with a boy named Sean, and they actually seemed like they might be friends later on in the book. And that was more like a happy feeling, so far.*

Dan: *So in most stories the mood doesn't stay the same all the way through.*

Vanessa: *No, it doesn't.*

Dan: *To read stories well, it seems to me we have to pay attention to the way the author is making us feel. Like "Oh my gosh, I get it, this part—depressing. Oh my gosh, this part is different—it's happy." Readers need to have a mood thermometer in their heads, where they notice how the feeling of the book changes.*

Vanessa: *So you can notice like when it goes from sad to happy. Where the feelings change.*

Dan: *Exactly. How would you like to do a reading project where you do a mood thermometer, and pay attention to places where the author is making you feel a certain way?*

Vanessa: *OK. I could show them on a timeline and see how it changes as the book goes on.*

Dan: *Great. Practicing paying attention to how the author wants you to feel in a story is something that will help you with* any *story, not just* Nory Ryan's Song.

Here our young reader leaves the conference with concrete work to do that involves tracking her own ideas across the book, rather than simply retelling. It's important to note that though the teacher took a very active role in naming things and prodding Vanessa to go further, the basic ideas came from *her*. In addition to doing work that will extend her understanding of the way stories develop, this student takes away the important message that she is able to use those retelling skills selectively—in the service of a good idea.

Easier Variation

Teaching Point: "Main characters feel different emotions as a story moves forward. To understand a narrative well, it's important for readers to pay attention to how and why their feelings change."

PROJECT: Keep a timeline of places where the main character's feelings change in important ways. At the end of the book, look across these changes and write a few lines about what you notice (see Figure 5.7).

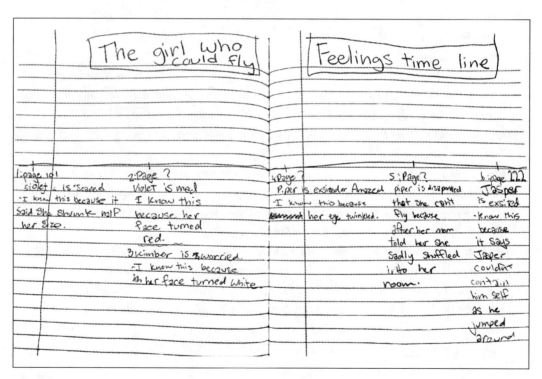

Figure 5.7 Fourth-grader Havana's "Feelings Timeline," tracking the emotions of main characters in *The Girl Who Could Fly*

More Difficult Variation

Teaching Point: "Authors of narratives have certain big ideas, or themes, that they want us to think about as we read a story. Usually these ideas develop from the beginning to the end. In order to think deeply about stories, readers need to stop and pay attention to places where the big idea seems to come up—and consider how one 'idea place' leads to the next."

Project: Keep a timeline of idea parts, jotting down a line or two each time about how it extends, or adds to, the theme. At the end, write about the big idea and how it develops across the text (see Figure 5.8).

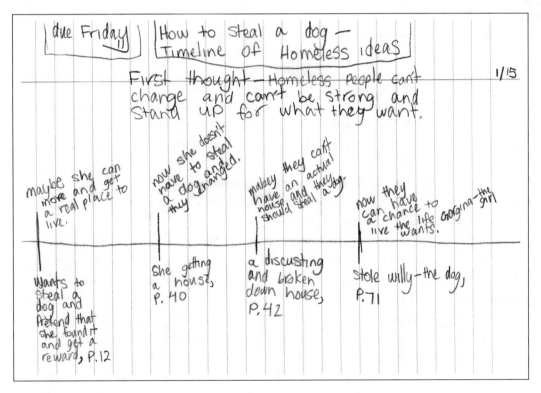

due Friday | How to Steal a dog —
Timeline of Homeless ideas

First thought—Homeless people can't change and can't be strong and stand up for what they want. 1/15

maybe she can move and get a real place to live.

now she doesn't have to steal a dog they changed.

mabey they can't have an actual house and they should steal a dog.

now they can have a chance to live the life Georgina—the girl wants.

Wants to steal a dog and Pretend that she found it and get a reward, P. 12

She getting a house, P. 40

a discusting and broken down house, P. 42

stole willy—the dog, P.71

Figure 5.8 Fifth-grader Sky's "Timeline of Homeless Ideas" about *How to Steal a Dog*

Helpful (and Not So Helpful) Connections (Narrative/Informational): Thinking About Your Thinking Conference

Teaching Point: "Readers often connect things they read to what they already know. Sometimes these connections help us understand the text better, and sometimes they don't. It's important to know which connections to stop and think about as we read and which ones might be distracting and *not* so helpful."

We may consider this type of conference when a student

- *references prior knowledge* when discussing a book
- *makes personal connections to text but is not clear* about how they do or don't add to understanding
- is *just learning to talk about what she does in her head* to understand a text.

Rationale

Ever since the publication of *Mosaic of Thought* (1997), schools around the country have been stressing text-to-self, text-to-text, and text-to-world connections. "I've even seen them mentioned on TV sitcoms," laments author Ellin Keene. "It makes me regret ever coming up with those phrases!"

To be clear, it's not that Ellin has changed her mind about the importance of making connections to text. "It's just that the phrases have become buzzwords," she explains. "People talk about them without thinking why they are important."

The truth is that children are pretty quick at figuring out the game, whatever the norms of the classroom. As a result, when teachers latched on to this idea, kids caught on—and students in classrooms everywhere began talking about their text-to-self, text-to-text, and text-to-world connections. What has gotten lost in the shuffle is the fact that not all connections are created equal. When a child is reading a Harry Potter book, to say "I went to a magic show once" may qualify as text-to-self, but it is not a connection that's likely to help the reader understand more deeply.

A Helpful (and Not So Helpful) Connections conference helps develop quality control in the mind of the reader. *Which connections are worth stopping to think about; which ones actually help me to understand? Which ones are not so helpful?* Skilled readers know when to stop and think about a text-to-self, text-to-text, or text-to-world observation and when such a connection is distracting. This sort of project gives students an opportunity to think critically about which is which.

Jordan's Conference (Fourth Grade):

Jordan is a girl who favors realistic fiction stories, usually about friendships and families. Not above and not below grade level, her comments about books tend to focus on characters' feelings. "She's pretty good at commenting on what is happening in the story," says Joanne Searle, her teacher at Manhattan New School, "but Jordan has a harder time talking about metacognitive stuff, her own reading process. That's difficult for any nine-year-old, but considering how tuned in she is to what's happening in her characters' heads, I think she might be ready."

> *Joanne: So you are pretty far into* Rules *by Cynthia Lord. What are you thinking about this book?*
>
> *Jordan: I like it. I have a lot of connections.*
>
> *Joanne: Can you say more about that?*
>
> *Jordan: For one thing, Catherine has a little brother and I have a little sister. So I know how it feels.*
>
> *Joanne: Interesting. Can you tell me more about your feeling connections?*
>
> *Jordan: Well, Catherine's brother David is autistic, so she has to take care of him a lot. There was this one part where she has to take him to therapy, but he wants to go to a video store instead. And she gets annoyed and impatient, like I do with my sister sometimes.*
>
> *Joanne: How did that connection help you understand the book better?*

Here is an example of a teacher using what she knows about a young reader to move the conference along. Going into the conference already aware of Jordan's ability to empathize, she goes straight to the next step, asking *how the connection helped her to understand.* Peter Johnston

(2004) writes about the importance of using language with students that positions them as insiders, capable of solving problems and thinking in sophisticated ways. Joanne's question sends a message to Jordan that of course she is capable of discussing her thinking—and as a result, her student rises to the occasion.

> **Jordan:** *Catherine was feeling impatient with David, even though she loves him. I have that same mix of feelings with my sister, so I know how Catherine feels. That's mostly what the book is about, her feelings about her brother, so the connection helps me understand what she's going through better.*
>
> **Joanne:** *That makes a lot of sense. I'm wondering, are there any connections that* don't *help you understand better?*

Interesting move here. Once students have expressed an idea, one way to push them to deepen their thinking is to ask about the opposite thing, the exception. Jordan has done a good job explaining how a connection helps her understand, so Joanne tests the waters by asking if there are ever times when it doesn't help.

> **Jordan:** *Hmm. Well, one way Catherine deals with stuff is by keeping a book where she sketches, and writes rules. I've never kept a book to write in and sketch in, so I don't really relate to that.*
>
> **Joanne:** *Would you say that some connections help you understand better than others?*
>
> **Jordan:** *Yes, definitely.*
>
> **Joanne:** *One thing readers need to be able to do is make connections to what they read—but it's important to know the difference between connections that help, and ones that don't. How would you like to do some work with* Rules *where you practice knowing the difference?*

In the end, the two decided on a project where Jordan listed several connections that helped her understand, and several that didn't (see Figures 5.9a and 5.9b). Joanne posted her work on a bulletin board for the rest of the class to see, thus sparking ongoing discussions in her class about helpful versus unhelpful connections. "It was Jordan's conference that started it," Joanne commented. "But now I feel like other kids are starting to be a little more selective about the connections they pay attention to."

The Next Conference Could Be . . .

Teaching Point: "Text-to-self, text-to-text, and text-to-world connections sometimes help us understand—but they may not all help in the same way. For example, some connections may

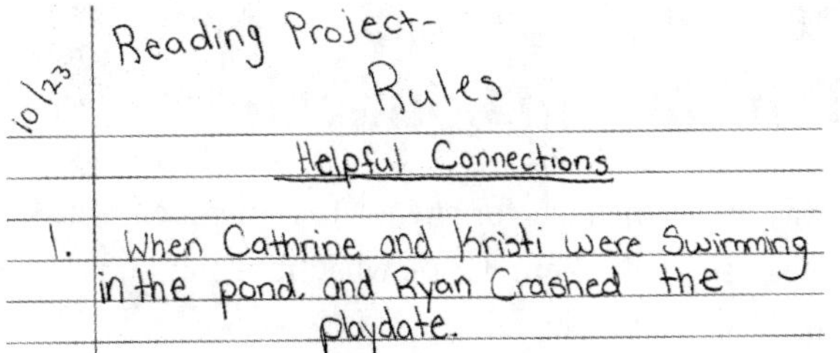

10/23

Reading Project–
Rules

Helpful Connections

1. When Cathrine and Kristi were swimming in the pond, and Ryan crashed the playdate.

2. Cathrine's little Brother (David) keeps annoying her, because he wants to go to the video store.

3. When Cathrine was annoyed at her little brother, and Ryan teased David by giving him a gum wraper with no gum in it. After David was crying, and Cathrine stuck up for him, and felt bad for him.

4. Cathrine is making word cards for Jason. He has autisum, so he can hear but not talk. He needs cards so he can point to words that he can't say.

5. Cathrine bought Jason a gutar. Cathrine and Jason then noticed they had →

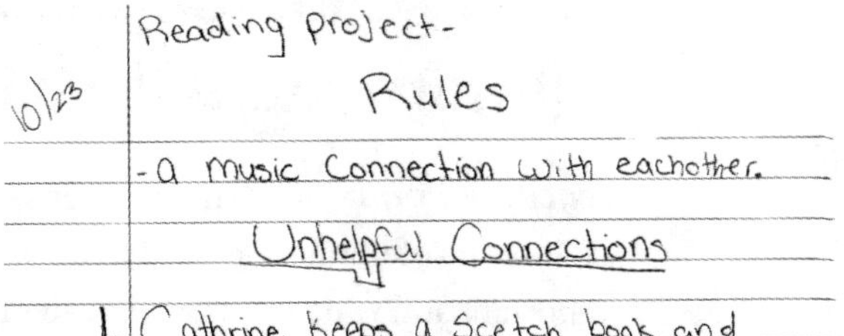

10/23

Reading Project–
Rules

- a music connection with eachother.

Unhelpful Connections

1. Cathrine keeps a scetch book and a rule book, that she writes in consistantly.
Why? This was an unhelpful connection because I have never kept a book that I scetch or write in. So I don't feel the feeling of what Cathrine does.

2. Cathrine got a next door naibor that she thought they would be friends.
Why? This was an unhelpful connection because I've never had a next door naibor, that I thought that we would be friends.

3. Cathrine's Brother goes to Ocupational Therapy.
Why? This was an unhelpful connection because my sister, or I have ever been to Ocupational Therapy.

Figures 5.9a and 5.9b Jordan's "Helpful (and Not So Helpful) Connections" work. To start, she noted places in the text with sticky notes, and then came up with these charts as a way of expressing her thinking.

describe a feeling we can relate to. Others might recall a type of story we've read before, thus allowing us to look for particular developments in the plot. In an informational text, a fact about what one animal eats may fit into what we know about another, similar animal. The more different ways we know that connections can help us think about what we read, the better we'll be able to use them to understand harder books."

PROJECT: Find *x* examples of places you made connections that helped you understand. Put them into three groups according to *how* they helped, e.g., feelings connections, similar-fact connections, type-of-story connections. See if you can discover some new categories!

Important to Remember, OK to Forget (Informational Text): Prioritizing Conference

Teaching Point: "Information books have way too many facts for anyone to remember them all. Readers of nonfiction need to develop strategies to help them decide what information is important and which facts are not so important."

We may consider this type of conference when a student
- *comments that a particular fact is interesting*
- is *new to the idea of prioritizing*
- is beginning to *learn note-taking skills*.

Rationale

One of the most common hurdles young readers face as they learn to read nonfiction is how to deal with information overload. Nonfiction for young readers, even in texts with few words, is often jam-packed with one fact after another. While text features such as captions and subject headings can be helpful, for an elementary-age child they sometimes feel like yet another variable to keep track of. The end result is that prioritizing becomes a major struggle.

An Important to Remember, OK to Forget conference is a concrete, entry-level approach that can help children develop strategies for determining importance.

Maria's Conference (Fourth Grade):

Maria is a struggling reader at River East School in Spanish Harlem. She tends to favor books with lots of pictures, and when she discusses her thinking about a text at all it is often in reference to the illustrations. Informational text is a particular struggle, due to her limited vocabulary and difficulty prioritizing. At the time of this conference, Maria was a few pages into a brightly colored picture book about sharks.

> *Dan: So Maria, this is a pretty interesting looking book. What made you choose it?*
> *Maria: It is interesting and I like sharks.*
> *Dan: What are you thinking about this book?*
> *Maria: (flips pages, then reads aloud) I'm thinking that "Sharks have more than 3,000 teeth, and they are razor sharp."*
> *Dan: Wow. That's a lot of teeth. What do you think about that?*

Maria: *It's a lot of teeth. And they are sharp so you wouldn't want to be bit by one.*

Dan: *I should think not. It was interesting how you added your own opinion to what you read, saying "you wouldn't want to be bit by one." Are you the kind of reader who usually comes up with her own ideas about things she reads?*

Maria: *Yes, especially about sharks, when the facts are interesting.*

Dan: *Hmm. So some facts are more interesting than others?*

Maria: *Some facts are more boring. They aren't as important.*

Dan: *Can you say more about that?*

Maria: *(flips pages again) Well, here's one. "Sharks do not have bones. Their skeletons are made of cartilage. Cartilage is the same type of tissue as your ear." Actually, the part about no bones is important, but I don't think the part about cartilage in the ear is important.*

Clearly, Maria's understanding was literal. Indeed, when first asked what she was thinking, she more or less randomly picked a part from the book and read it aloud. It would have been easy to give up and jump in with a teacher-determined agenda at this point, but volunteering a reaction ("Wow. That's a lot of teeth") and asking for one in return paid off (". . . you wouldn't want to be bit by one"). Peter Johnston (2004) reminds us that sometimes the most effective affirmation is to name a behavior the student herself might not realize she is doing effectively (". . . you added

your own opinion about what you read"). Once Maria heard this, her confidence seemed to increase and she began to talk about interesting and boring facts—a natural lead-in to a discussion about which were important to remember and which were OK to forget.

> *Dan: It sounds like you are saying that sharks having no bones is important to remember, but the part about cartilage is not so important.*
>
> *Maria: That's right. It's boring.*
>
> *Dan: Maria, you are doing some important work here. Information books have too many facts for anyone to remember all of them, so it's important to decide which ones are important to remember, and which are OK to forget. How would you like to do a project where you practice deciding which facts to remember and which to forget?*
>
> *Maria: I decide myself?*
>
> *Dan: You are the reader, so you decide. How will you know which are which?*
>
> *Maria: I'll forget the boring ones and remember the important ones.*
>
> *Dan: Great. I'm going to challenge you to find one fact on each page that is important to remember and one that's OK to forget. You can mark the "remember" facts with blue sticky notes and the "OK to forget" ones with pink sticky notes. Does that make sense?*
>
> *Maria: Yes. I'm going to get so many facts.*
>
> *Dan: And doing this work in your shark book will help you practice making important decisions about which facts are the ones to remember, but also which ones you don't have to think about. That's something that will help you in any nonfiction book, not just this one.*

The important thing to remember here is that, especially for our most struggling readers, the priority should be to teach the reader, not the book. Whether the fact about cartilage is critical or not is not the point. For a passive reader like Maria to learn to actively make decisions about what is important is a huge step.

The Next Conference Could Be . . .

Teaching Point: "As readers of information books make decisions about which facts are important to remember and which are OK to forget, they stop to think about the reasons why. In order to do this well, we need to have ideas about what makes one fact more important than another."

Project: Find three facts in each chapter (*or one on each page—however many makes sense for the specific book and the individual reader*) that are important to remember, and one that it is OK to forget. For each one, jot down a few words about why you made your decision (i.e., "It's important/not important *because . . .*").

Two-Way Street (Narrative/Informational): Paying Attention to How Things Develop Conference

Teaching Point: "One important way readers keep track of stories is to make predictions. To do this well, they must think of all that's happened so far, what the characters' personalities are like, and any other information that will help to guess what comes next."

We may consider this type of conference when a student

- offers an *explanation for a prediction*
- comments on *reasons a character said or did something*
- is *determined to stick with a particularly challenging text*
- *comments on different possibilities* for how a story might unfold.

Rationale

Elementary and middle school readers are famous for sticking with their first impressions. If a character seems mean at first—even if the whole point of the story is how they secretly have a heart of gold—at the end of the book, many young readers will still call them mean. Revising their ideas as they read is something they must be *taught* to do; developmentally, children at this age are only just learning to be more flexible thinkers. (For this same reason, many well-meaning teachers tear their hair out trying to get students to revise their writing!)

Often it is helpful to give readers of this age concrete, baby-step strategies to help them learn to see possibilities beyond their original idea. A Two-Way Street conference teaches one such strategy.

Donovan's Conference (Fourth Grade):

Like many upper elementary students, Donovan's reading priorities were very much about keeping up with current, popular books—and this was the year of *The Lightning Thief*. Though a grade-level reader, the book was slightly above his independent level. Donovan was not deterred; he desperately wanted to tackle it. "Most of his reading responses up until now had been about characters and relationships," his teacher Jamie Kushner explained, "though in class discussions he occasionally took a chance on talking about bigger ideas. And he was so motivated to get through this book! I didn't want to burst his bubble and suggest something easier."

Jamie: So Donovan, what are you working on?

Donovan: I'm reading Percy Jackson, Lightning Thief, *the first book. My mom influenced me to read these books, and sometimes I don't get what's going on, so then I like, read it over. So that's one of my goals that I'm trying to do, and then I understand the book more.*

Jamie: Can you show me a part you didn't understand, but then when you reread it helped you understand better?

Donovan: Right here. They got stuck in a car and Percy just heard that he was being guarded from evil Gods, and I didn't understand if he knew completely or if he thinks his Mom is lying. He wants to be positive, and I thought he was already positive, so it was confusing. And then I figured out that he still wanted to figure out if his Mom was lying because he wasn't positive that his Mom was a God and they were protecting him from evil Gods. And his teacher has legs of a goat now, and he thinks it's like a dream, and then I read it over and somewhere it said that it wasn't a dream, and that's where I got it.

Jamie: What about this part do you think was confusing to you?

Donovan: If Percy was positive that his Mom and his teacher were actually Gods protecting him from evil Gods, or if he thought they were just tricking him and it's a dream.

Every now and then you hit one of those jackpot conferences where the child articulates a direction right away. Here, as if on cue, Donovan speaks of his goal to get through the confusing parts in *The Lightning Thief* by rereading. Without missing a beat, Jamie asks if he can *show her a part* to illustrate his point.

Before settling on the teaching point in a conference-based reading project, it is often helpful to ask students to point to a place in the book that illustrates their idea. This serves the dual purpose of testing the student's ability to find evidence and also gives the teacher a chance to watch the child *chunk* the text, i.e., figure out exactly where in the story something happened. Some readers flip the pages randomly; others think *hmm, it was somewhere near the beginning but not in the first few pages—* and approximate about where they think it might be. Watching what kids do as they find a part gives us a bit of a window into how they are putting the story together in their minds.

And now the naming.

Jamie: So it sounds to me like you are doing something really important. Aside from the fact that you are realizing when you're confused and rereading, you are also coming up with ideas in your mind. You're stopping and saying "wait a second, that doesn't make sense," and then coming up with different possibilities of what it could be. What were the different possibilities you said?

Donovan: That he was just dreaming and none of this is actually happening, or if this is really happening and they are protecting him from evil Gods.

Jamie: Is that something you do a lot as a reader? Do you come up with questions in your mind, and think "well, it could be this, or it could be this, or it could be this"?

Donovan: Not in books that are easy for me but in books like this one, where I'm challenging myself.

Jamie: It seems to me that you are figuring out what's going on by tracking those possibilities as you continue to read, gathering information. Like in one part it seems as if it's a dream and you tuck that away in your head, but in another part it seems like they are Gods and they are protecting him, and you're putting that in another box. So what I'd like to challenge you to do is when you find yourself following an idea in your head, and having two different possibilities of what it could be—two-way street parts—keep track of it. In other words, you say this is evidence that Percy Jackson's mom is a God and she's protecting him and this is evidence that it's a dream. And you see where it goes.

Donovan: So I'm writing down the two possibilities and then writing the proof that I have for one possibility to show it's true?

Jamie: You explained that way better than I did. That's exactly what I want you to do. So you have options about how you could do this. What works best for you? Do sticky notes work well, or is it more helpful to work in your reading notebook?

Donovan: The reading notebook works better for me.

Jamie: OK. Donovan, this is really important work. Doing this will help you practice thinking carefully about parts where the story could go different ways so those parts don't confuse you as your books get harder.

Following this exchange, Jamie and Donovan agreed on a T-chart format, how many "two-idea" spots he would record, and when the project would be due. It's interesting to note that Jamie gave her student a choice of *how* to keep track of his thinking, allowing the learner to match his purpose to a particular format. More important, he walked away with concrete work to do that helped him practice considering more than one way a story can develop (see Figure 5.10).

The Next Conference Could Be . . .

Teaching Point: "(Reading like a writer conference) To keep readers interested, authors will sometimes lead us to predict that a story is going in one direction but then make something else happen. It can be interesting to think back and identify exactly where in the story the author has tricked us—and *why*. Reflecting on how writers plant clues can help us not just with future reading, but also with our own writing."

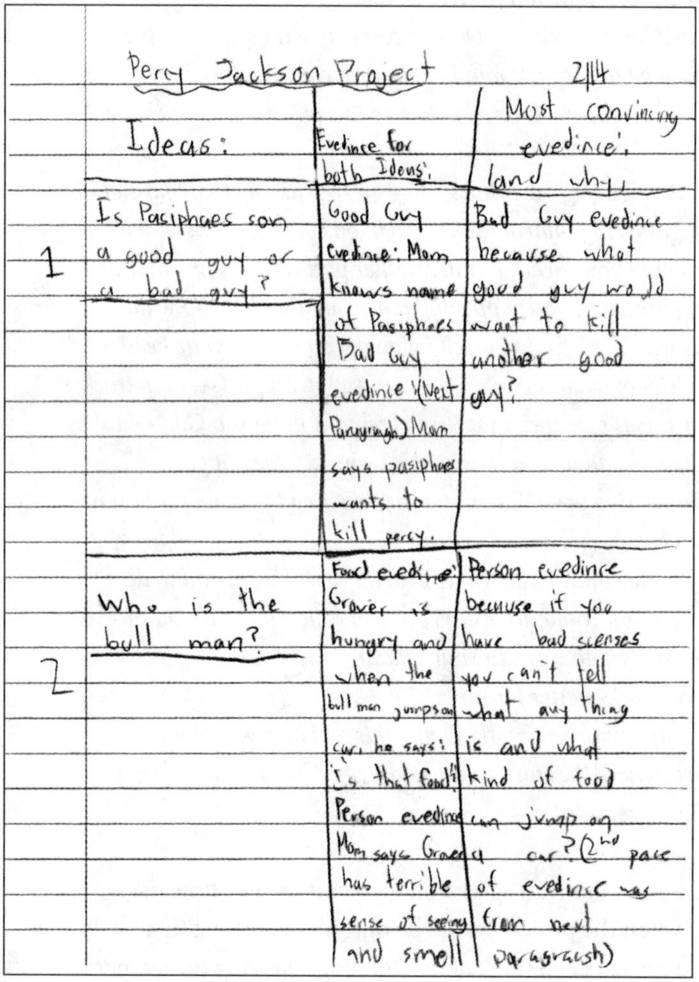
Percy Jackson Project 2/14

	Ideas:	Evedince for both Ideas:	Most convincing evedince, and why,
1	Is Pasiphaes son a good guy or a bad guy?	Good Guy evedince: Mom knows name of Pasiphaes Bad Guy evedince (Next Paragraph) Mom says pasiphaes wants to kill percy.	Bad Guy evedince because what good guy wold want to kill another good guy?
2	Who is the bull man?	Food evedince: Graver is hungry and when the bull man jumps on car, he says: Is that food?! Person evedince Mom says Graver has terrible sense of seeing and smell	Person evedince because if you have bad scenses you can't tell what any thing is and what kind of food can jump on a car? (2nd pace of evedince was from next paragraph)

Figure 5.10 Donovan's "Two-Way Street" chart. The student decided on how to set up the chart himself, recording evidence for each possibility and then his thinking about which was more convincing.

Project: Find *x* places in the next four chapters where something happened that was different from what you expected. Then look back and identify at least one part from earlier in the text that tricked you into thinking something else would happen. Write a few lines about how the author tricked you and why you think he did that.

Easier Variation

Teaching Point: "Sometimes we predict a story will go a certain way, but the author surprises us. When something happens that is different from what they expect, readers think back to earlier parts in the book that explain the surprise. Connecting parts from before to explain places where we are surprised is one strategy for understanding a story more deeply."

Project: Find two places in the book where something happened that was different from what you predicted. Mark one with a blue sticky note and the other with a yellow sticky note, and write a few words about why it was surprising. Then, for each part, find a place from earlier in the book that connects to the surprise and mark it with the same color sticky note. Write a few words about how this part connects to the unexpected event.

Places That Are Confusing (Narrative/ Informational): Two Thinking About Your Thinking Conferences

Teaching Point: "No matter how good a reader you are, there are always going to be some parts in a text that are more confusing for you than other parts. Most people have certain *types* of things in books that they know are especially hard for *them*—where they need to pay special attention. It's helpful to know which sorts of things can be confusing to *you* as a reader, and what strategies to use when you come to such places."

We may consider this type of conference when a student

- *admits to having difficulty with a certain passage*
- is *just learning to talk about what she does in her head* to understand a text
- identifies a part in the text where she realized something, e.g., *"it began to make sense."*

Rationale

Many students are embarrassed to admit when they do not understand something they've read. Their idea of being a good reader is that things come easily and you always "get what it's about." The notion of reader as problem solver—a person who works to figure things out—is largely lost once students leave the earliest grades.

As teachers, we bear some of the responsibility for this attitude. Peter Johnston (2012) cites sobering research on the effect of feedback to students that results in fixed mindsets—a reluctance to take risks for fear of failure. If we want students to be willing to admit something is difficult, let alone be excited to take on new challenges, then it is important to make it the cool thing in reading class to talk about how we solve such problems. A Places That Are Confusing conference is a way to acknowledge the importance of working to figure things out. It is also a vote of confidence to the student—sending the message that you know they can do it.

Nate's Conference (Fifth Grade):

Nate is an avid reader who flies through books at a rapid clip. "While he was assessed at slightly above grade level," writes Leslie Profeta, his teacher at Manhattan New School, "he reads so fast that it affects his comprehension. It's that old 'I can read faster than the other kid' thing. There's a competitiveness to his reading that gets in the way of deeper thinking." Like many boys his age, Nate prefers funny books, action or adventure stories, and nonfiction on topics of high interest (e.g., baseball, video games). At the time of this conference, *Hatchet* was a popular book in his class. "Nate gets excited about what he reads, but he needs to practice slowing down to discuss his thinking. I think he picked up this book because he didn't want to be left out," comments Leslie. "When it turned out to be harder than he expected, he didn't want to give up. I felt like it was important to support him in trying."

> **Leslie:** *This is a different sort of book than you usually read. What are you thinking about it?*
> **Nate:** *I'm on page 56. I think it's a really good book. It's challenging for me.*
> **Leslie:** *Can you say more about that?*
> **Nate:** *Well, it's challenging because sometimes the story is slow, and sometimes it's fast.*
> **Leslie:** *Interesting. Can you find me an example of a slow part and also a fast part?*

Let's stop and look at Leslie's decisions up until now. Nate volunteers a thought, however vague, and his teacher does *not* ask him to elaborate by encouraging him to say more—*yet*. Drawing on her knowledge of this particular reader, she creates conditions for success by first asking for a concrete example. "Knowing Nate," she explains, "I thought it would be easier to explain what he meant if he had actual examples in front of him. He can be very impatient, and tends to do better with a particular part from the book to talk off of."

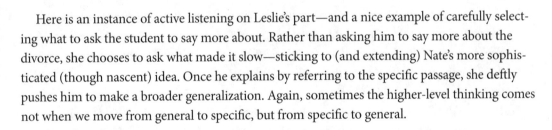

> **Nate:** *(flipping through the book) Here's a part that was slow. It's about Brian's parents' divorce.*
>
> **Leslie:** *What makes it slow?*
>
> **Nate:** *Well, it's like he's just talking about one thing for a really long time. He's thinking stuff about the divorce, not saying stuff.*
>
> **Leslie:** *Hmm. So are thinking parts slower than saying parts?*
>
> **Nate:** *Yes, definitely.*

Here is an instance of active listening on Leslie's part—and a nice example of carefully selecting what to ask the student to say more about. Rather than asking him to say more about the divorce, she chooses to ask what made it slow—sticking to (and extending) Nate's more sophisticated (though nascent) idea. Once he explains by referring to the specific passage, she deftly pushes him to make a broader generalization. Again, sometimes the higher-level thinking comes not when we move from general to specific, but from specific to general.

> **Leslie:** *Can you show me a place that feels faster?*
>
> **Nate:** *Right here on page 11. The part where the pilot dies of a heart attack.*
>
> **Leslie:** *Why is that faster?*
>
> **Nate:** *Because there's more action and not so much thinking.*
>
> **Leslie:** *So Nate, I am thinking back to what you said a minute ago, about the book being challenging because of the slow and fast parts. Can you say more about that now?*
>
> **Nate:** *Well, the slow parts are harder for me. I get confused when there's thinking and it stays on one thing for a long time. It's easier when there's more action. But I still like the book.*
>
> **Leslie:** *Nate, what you have just done is really important work. Every reader has things that are hard for them, but not everyone is willing to admit it. To read harder books well, the trick is being able to recognize what those things are when you get to them, and*

knowing some things you can do about it. Would you be willing to talk about this with the rest of the class? I think others can learn from you.
Nate: *Thanks. Sure!*

Leslie has done a couple of important things worth calling out in these last exchanges. First of all, she has referred back to Nate's exact comments from earlier in the conference. There is no way this student doesn't know his teacher is hanging on every word, thus pushing him to say more and be more thoughtful. At the same time, she is taking time to name and affirm what he is thinking, making special note of his willingness to admit when things are difficult. Nate the competitive reader now feels like there is social capital to being the one who encourages others to think about confusing parts in a text. But before ending the conference, it is time for Leslie to give her student some meaningful work to do, based on his own ideas.

Leslie: *So what do you do when you come to those hard parts?*
Nate: *Sometimes I read it again. Sometimes I skip paragraphs that are confusing and don't seem that important to the story. And sometimes I just keep going and it starts to make sense.*
Leslie: *How would you like to do a reading project where you practice noticing places that are confusing, and thinking what to do about them? For example, you just told me how slow parts that talk about one thing for a long time can be difficult. Do you suppose those are the only sorts of parts that are hard for you?*
Nate: *No. There are probably others.*
Leslie: *Would it be interesting work to look for more confusing parts and see what other sorts of things you need to pay attention to? Then you can share what you learn with the rest of the class.*
Nate: *That would be cool.*
Leslie: *How about if you find one part from each chapter that was confusing for some reason, jot down what made it hard, and then say what you did about it?*
Nate: *OK. How many chapters?*
Leslie: *What do you think?*
Nate: *I'd say maybe for the next five chapters.*
Leslie: *Great—and then you can write a few lines about what you've noticed, in your reading notebook. This work will help you practice paying attention to the sorts of things that get in the way of your understanding, and coming up with strategies for what to do about them. And getting good at that will help you read other hard books, not just Hatchet.*

In the end, what started out as an abstract conversation about fix-it strategies ended with concrete work to push a young reader to think about his thinking. "That conference fit neatly into my goals for Nate," reflected Leslie. He realized that he was having trouble understanding areas of the text where the character was thinking to himself. It led into class conversations about how you can read certain 'plot' parts quickly without missing important ideas, but there are other parts that warrant slower, more deliberate reading, with pauses—such as when the character is thinking to himself. Those areas are more likely to relate to the theme, or the author's point."

The Next Conference Could Be . . .

Teaching Point: "Readers need a repertoire of 'fix-it' strategies to call on when a text gets confusing. Once we become aware of our personal comprehension hurdles (and develop some ideas of how to get past them), the next step is to look at the opposite end of the spectrum—passages where we realize we are *not* confused. Which sentences, passages, paragraphs, are the ones where a light bulb goes off and we understand something we didn't understand before? It's important for a reader to stop and think carefully about these passages."

PROJECT:
VERSION ONE (*Easier*) Find one passage in each chapter where something important became clear. Jot down what you realized and why.

VERSION TWO (*More advanced*) For each light bulb moment, make a generalization, i.e., name the *type* of passage it was. For example, in a narrative we may look for parts where friends disagree or where an older character gives advice to a younger one; in nonfiction, it could be passages that start with *However*, *Most importantly*, or *On the other hand*.

Hannah's Conference (Narrative, Seventh Grade):

Hannah is a complicated reader. "She's one of the strongest in the class," reports Shannon Potts, her ELA teacher at the

Special Music School. "Hannah placed well above grade level on the reading inventory I gave at the beginning of the year. But mostly she plays it safe with what I'd call 'girl' books—you know, romances or coming of age stories with teen girl protagonists. She and I agreed it would be a good idea for her to challenge herself."

At the time of this conference, at her teacher's recommendation, Hannah was struggling through *Extremely Loud and Incredibly Close* by Jonathan Safran Foer, a complex, multi-layered book about a boy whose father dies in the 9/11 attacks. By the student's own admission, the novel was beyond her usual independent reading level, and she was feeling frustrated. Shannon wasn't sure where to go in a conference with Hannah or even whether she should urge her to continue, so she asked me to try.

> *Dan: So Hannah, Ms. Potts tells me you are feeling frustrated with this book.*
> *Hannah: Well, I've been reading it for a long time and it's pretty confusing.*
> *Dan: Do you want to keep going with it?*
> *Hannah: Yes. I really like some parts, and I don't want to give up. I want to figure out what to do to understand it.*
> *Dan: Can you say more about the confusing parts?*
> *Hannah: One example is that there's not always punctuation, so you don't always know who's talking.*
> *Dan: Can you show me an example of a part that was really confusing?*

Interestingly, Hannah did not choose a passage illustrating the lack of punctuation she'd just mentioned. Instead, she flipped to a part where the text broke out of conventional narrative structure to include a letter written by one of the characters. This was useful information. Although she did not say so explicitly, choosing this passage indicated her awareness that what made the book confusing went further than just knowing who was talking.

> *Hannah: Here's a part where it goes to a letter, and I'm not sure how it fits. The letter is from his grandfather, who isn't even alive. There are other parts, too, where I'm not sure how it connects.*
> *Dan: I can see how that would be confusing. What do you think about that?*
> *Hannah: I'm not sure. But Oskar, the kid who is the main character, has autism, so maybe it's supposed to be confusing.*
> *Dan: Hmm. You just said two things I'd like to know more about. For one, that the parts are not connecting—and also the idea that it's supposed to be confusing. Can you tell me more about those things?*

On one level, our young reader seemed to be grabbing at straws in attempting to explain her struggles. On the other hand, Hannah had identified two important notions related to her confusion—that things were not obviously connected, and the idea that maybe the author *wanted* it to be confusing. As the teacher in the conference, it occurred to me that maybe what she needed was some help in putting those two things together. Asking the question seemed to spark something.

> **Hannah:** *Well, the writer obviously isn't writing the story in a regular way. It sort of skips around weirdly, like Oskar's mind with the autism. So I guess you have to figure out what thing goes with what other thing if you want to understand it.*
>
> **Dan:** *Are there parts where you are reading along and realize "Wow, this part goes with something from before," and you feel less confused?*
>
> **Hannah:** *Yes. (flips to a page in the book) Here there is a letter from the grandmother that sort of connects back to the letter from the grandfather.*
>
> **Dan:** *Hannah, I think you are on to something. When books are especially challenging, one thing a reader can do is flag parts where it doesn't quite make sense and be patient, in case it's supposed to be confusing. Then you can be on the lookout for parts that connect back, which may explain the confusing part.*
>
> **Hannah:** *Maybe. I never thought of that.*
>
> **Dan:** *Would you like to do a reading project where you practice this with* Extremely Loud and Incredibly Close?

Here was a case where the teacher's role was to pick out parts of the student's emergent thinking and name them in order to help push her to the next level. It is unlikely that Hannah would have come to this realization on her own; at the same time, the genesis of the project absolutely came from her own ideas.

Here is the work she turned in a few days later, recording points of confusion and moments of clarity (she calls them "resolution") that connect back to the earlier passages.

Hannah

Humanities 7

Confusion and Resolution

CONFUSION

» I am confused about why this mysterious lady starts crying after the man writes that he can't speak. Did this lady even know the man? p. 31

» At this part, I almost thought Oskar's dad was actually alive. How was his name on the paper at the art store, when he had been dead for longer than the time the paper was out (as I learned from Oskar's encounter with the art store lady)? p. 49

» There are a lot of things I was confused about when I was reading this anonymous letter. Who was the letter from, why was it so private, and how did Oskar get it? My main question was do I have to pay attention to this for later on in the story? Did it connect to the story? Was it important? p. 75

» I am confused about why the grandmother is telling Oskar all of this information about her marriage in the letter. Even though she says "you are the only one I trust, Oskar," why does Oskar need to know? Does he want to know? pp. 84–85

» I didn't know what E.S.P. was, so this page became confusing because I didn't understand what Oskar and Abby Black were talking about. E.S.P. is extrasensory perception, sensing something with your mind, rather than see, hear, touch, taste, or smell. p. 94

» I wondered why Oskar associated the picture of an elephant crying and their conversation. If they were talking about elephants communicating, why wouldn't the picture be of something else related to the elephant communication? Sometimes the pictures in the book don't always make sense to me. p. 95

» I am confused about how the letter from Stephen Hawking has anything to do with the places it pops up. Does Oskar get multiple letters from Stephen Hawking that are not personal, or does Oskar continue to think of one letter from Stephen Hawking at different times? The letter comes up on p. 12, p. 106, p. 200, and p. 242.

» There are so many letters in this book, and I have no idea how they got to Oskar. Are they specifically for him, or did he end up with them by mistake? On page 111, there is a letter about Dresden, Anna, and rules. I don't know who the letter is from, how Oskar got it, and how it relates to the story.

» On page 113, this person who didn't speak seemed to be talking in the book format. I was confused if this person was actually mute, because the book conversation format makes it seem like this person is talking.

» Why is this lady saying "My eyes are crummy"? Is she trying to get out of writing down her life story? What is she trying to accomplish? p. 119

» Why does this man feel he has failed his wife on page 124? When she asks him to read her life story, why does he say "I have failed you"? What was wrong?

» ". . . Toothpaste and The Minch were my best friends," p. 234 confused me because I thought that Oskar didn't like The Minch and Toothpaste. Weren't they mean to him? When/how did they become friends?

» On page 243, Oskar gives himself a bruise after ordering coffee with coffee ice cubes. "I went to the bathroom and gave myself a bruise." I know he gives himself bruises when he is feeling upset, but was he so upset that the coffee store didn't have coffee ice cubes that he hurt himself? What is the significance of a bruise in this particular situation?

» **Who is Anna?** Why does she keep coming up? Did the grandfather like Anna and then marry Oskar's grandmother?

» Why does the grandfather say that Oskar looks like Anna? I was confused because I thought that Anna was not Oskar's grandmother. How could Oskar look like Anna if he wasn't related to her? p. 276

» In this letter, the person who is writing asks "How could you?" How could you what? This confused me because I didn't know the topic of the letter. p. 310

» In the same letter, it seems like the letter will answer the question, "How could you?" but instead it makes it more confusing. The book says "He wrote, You were happy when I was away," which implies that this person writing the answer to the question "How could you," but then another question is asked. "How could you think that?" So I am not really sure if the two questions are a continuation of each other, or if there are two *different* questions being asked. p. 310

RESOLUTION

» "'It was probably manipulated in Photoshop,'" p. 96 resolves my confusion about why and how there was a crying elephant in Abby Black's apartment.

» The red writing on pages 208–216 was an example of a letter that Oskar's father had edited. At first, I though someone had marked up the book. Usually, Oskar's father had marked up newspapers, but this was a letter from Oskar's grandfather, Thomas' father.

» Anna was the girl who kissed Oskar's grandmother! Anna and the grandpa were having a sleepover. p. 228

» Thomas is the grandfather's name also! "'Who are you?' He went to the next page and wrote, 'My name is Thomas.'" p. 237

» Now that I know that the grandfather's name is Thomas, I know that the person who wrote on the art pads was Thomas Sr. Now everything makes sense; the art store employee was not giving false information when she said the art pads had only been out for a couple of weeks, and now I can dismiss my doubts about Oskar's father being dead.

» On page 256, I now understand why the pixelated pictures of a falling man keep coming up. Oskar found them on a Portuguese website and continues to zoom in because he thinks it is his dad.

» Also on page 256, the grandpa probably understands what Oskar is saying when he translates English words into German.

» One more thing on page 256 is when Oskar continues to talk to the grandfather about the grandfather and it just makes sense.

» Now I know how old the grandfather is. Pages 260 and 261 show the age in his hands. I thought he was younger since Oskar is a young kid.

» The Nothing Places mentioned in letters were actually with Oskar's grandfather and grandmother, not Oskar's dad. p. 274

» When the grandfather is explaining the materials he bought at the art store, that is when he wrote his name on the pads. He tested all of the materials, including pens. p. 274

» There was no specific page, but at some point I realized that Anna was Oskar's grandmother's sister. I also realized throughout many pages that she was pregnant, then died in a Dresden WWII bombing.

Domino Effect (Narrative): Paying Attention to How Things Develop/Connecting the Dots Conference

Teaching Point: "It's important to notice how a character's thoughts and feelings can lead to an action—or sometimes how an action leads to a thought or feeling. It's like dominoes; one thing causes another thing. Stopping and thinking about how one thing leads to another can help a reader understand a story better."

We may consider this type of conference when a student

- mostly retells but is *beginning to express opinions within the retell*
- comments on *reasons a character said or did something* in the story
- notices how *actions or feelings connect* in a text.

Rationale

When a teacher asks a student what he or she is thinking about a text, the go-to response is often a retell. In truth, this is our fault; from kindergarten forward, the first question children usually hear in school after reading is "Can you tell me what happened?" Young readers learn early that if they give a blow-by-blow account of the events in a story, they are off the hook.

Of course a retell can be valuable assessment, especially when working with struggling readers. But what's in it for the student? From a child's point of view, there is little apparent purpose to retelling, beyond pleasing the grown-up. When most of us read something we are excited about, our first reaction is not to call a friend and go through everything that happened in chapter two. We retell when there is a reason to do so—to give evidence to explain our thinking. This same logic may be applied to students. It is the job of the teacher to give children opportunities to recount events in a story in the service of expressing a thought or opinion. In this way, they feel a sense of purpose—and we get much the same assessment information as from a straight retell.

A Domino Effect conference can be a good starting place as children begin to move beyond passive retelling. By thinking about how one thing leads to another, they are at once recalling (and connecting) details in sequence, but also making their own judgments about how parts of the text are related. The teacher gets to see how much the reader has understood, and the student gets a chance to retell for a reason.

Aidan's Conference (Fourth Grade):

Aidan is your basic nine-year-old-boy reader. His favorite types of books are fantasy adventure (with lots of action, fights, etc.) and funny stuff (preferably with a bit of bathroom humor). By and large, his reading responses have involved recounting parts of the story and describing them as "cool" or "funny," without elaborating further. "He's pretty much reading on grade level," explains his teacher Jamie Kushner, "but I'm a little worried about how he'll do with harder books. Aidan definitely has feelings about what he reads, and does OK expressing them in whole-class read-alouds, but he has a hard time doing it in his reading responses."

Going into the conference, her goal was to help Aidan name an idea or reaction that he could continue thinking about, and help him find a format for keeping track that might push him to say more.

> **Jamie:** *Hmm.* Big Nate Flips Out *is a pretty dramatic title. What are you thinking about this one?*

> **Aidan:** *I like it. Nate gets in trouble a lot, so it's pretty funny.*
>
> **Jamie:** *Interesting. I remember that in your last book,* Middle School, The Worst Years of Your Life, *you talked about how funny it was when the characters got in trouble. Can you say more about that?*
>
> **Aidan:** *Well, in both books they get in trouble*

from doing things they aren't supposed to do. I guess I like stories where characters break rules. Rule breaking is appealing.

Note Jamie's deft move here, drawing on her knowledge of Aidan's recent reading history. Since the objective was to get him to elaborate on his thinking, it made sense to move away from just talking about *Big Nate Flips Out*, which would likely have resulted in a retell of whatever plot point he remembered from today's reading. By asking Aidan to say something about how his current book connected to the last one, she pushed him to say something that couldn't be said in a single word. And when Aidan volunteered "I find rule breaking appealing," she hit pay dirt.

Jamie: Rule breaking is appealing, huh? Say more about that.
Aidan: Nate always wants to do things that are against the rules. So he always thinks about it, and then he does it, and something happens, and it's funny.
Jamie: Wow. He always thinks about it. I'd love to hear more about that.
Aidan: Well, sometimes he thinks about it after. He doesn't always think about it first.
Jamie: Say more.
Aidan: Like there's this one part where the camera gets lost. First it gets lost, and then someone has to take responsibility. So then he thinks about it.
Jamie: Sounds as though there are action parts, like where the camera gets lost, and then there are thinking parts, like where Nate thinks about who is responsible.
Aidan: Yeah.
Jamie: How do the thought parts and action parts connect to make it funny?
Aidan: They are related. I mean sometimes thought parts lead up to action parts. Or action parts lead up to thought parts. Like stuff happens, and then characters think about it. Like losing the camera is an action part, and taking responsibility is a thought part. They go together, and then it's funny.

Let's look at how this conference has unfolded. Before leaping in with her own agenda, Jamie asked Aidan several times—four, to be exact—to "say more about that." It's important to recognize, though, that she hasn't been passive during these exchanges; each time she has isolated one thing (i.e., "rule breaking is appealing," "he always thinks about it") to ask him to say more *about*. Once Aidan has arrived at a bigger idea, she pulls out of "say more about that" mode, names what she is hearing (i.e., "Sounds as though there are action parts, like where the camera gets lost, and then there are thinking parts"), and asks a more directive question.

> *Jamie: So the thought parts and action parts make a domino effect—one leads to the other.*
> *Aidan: Sort of. Yeah.*
> *Jamie: Aidan, you are really on to something here. One thing that readers need to be able to do to understand why things happen in stories is notice how character's thoughts connect to their actions, and vice versa. If you get good at that, you'll be able to read harder and harder books. How would you like to do a project where you practice paying attention to connections between thoughts and actions?*
> *Aidan: That would be fun.*
> *Jamie: OK. Let's make a goal. About how many examples of thought and action connections do you think you can find between now and the end of the book?*
> *Aidan: Hmm. Maybe ten. At least.*
> *Jamie: Great. And when can you get it done by?*
> *Aidan: I'd say three days.*
> *Jamie: OK, so it'll be due Friday. And when you are done, write a few lines in your notebook about how noticing thought and action connections helped you understand the book better.*
> *Aidan: OK.*
> *Jamie: Aidan, I think doing this work will help you practice seeing how one thing in a book causes other things to happen, like dominoes—and that's something that will help you in any book.*

To wrap up the conference, Jamie has not only affirmed Aidan's thinking, but has also given him language to remember it by—a "domino effect"—and articulated *why* this is an important strategy for a reader to practice. Lastly, she has enlisted the student in setting his own goals, both for the number of examples and when it's due. In the end, Jamie played a pivotal role in facilitating Aidan's thinking—not telling him what to think about (see Figure 5.11).

The Next Conference Could Be . . .

Teaching Point: "Main characters in stories want something. It's not always obvious what they want. It could be an actual thing, like a new bike or a place to live; or it could be more of a

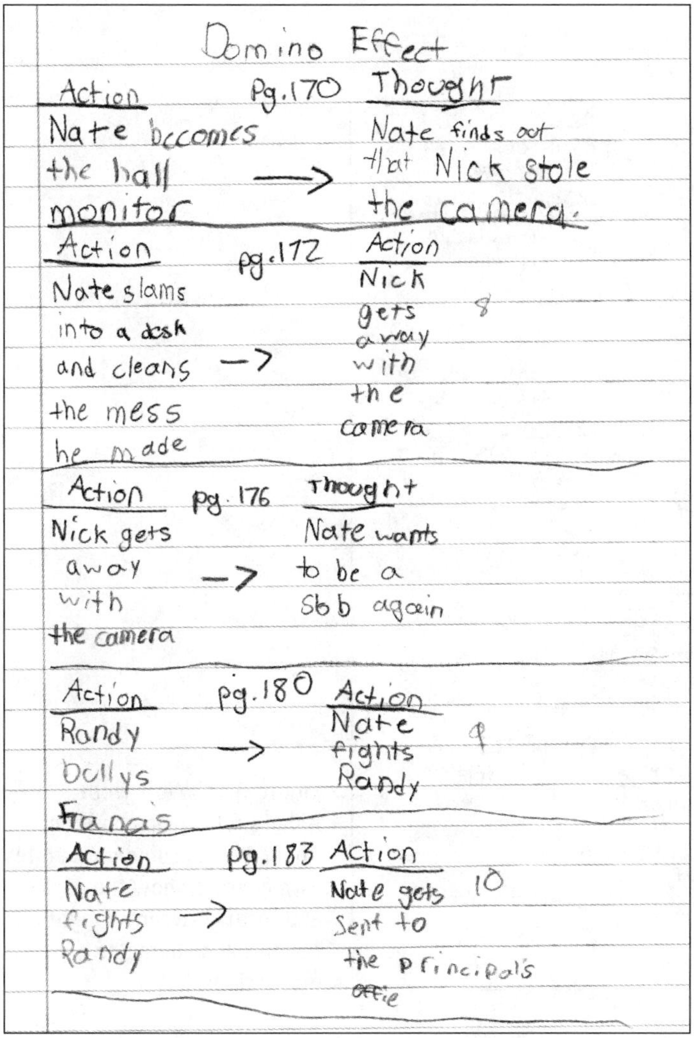

Figure 5.11 Aidan's "Action-Thought" chart. Notable is the fact that Jamie did not dictate the format; Aidan decided on the T-chart-with-arrows approach on his own as the best way to express his thinking. It's interesting, too, to see how he discovered along the way that actions can sometimes lead to other actions, rather than always thought to action—a revision to his original idea.

feeling, like wanting to fit in or wanting a friend. What they want is sometimes called *character motivation*. Thoughts and actions in stories are connected to one another—and both of them are connected to what the character wants, i.e., character motivation."

PROJECT: Find *x* examples of places where a character's actions and thoughts connect to what he or she wants. (see Figure 5.12).

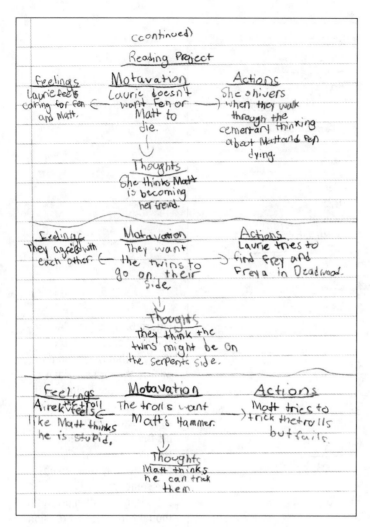

Figure 5.12 Work from Aidan's follow-up conference. Again, he has come up with his own chart to show the back and forth between thoughts, actions, and character motivations.

More Difficult Variations

Teaching Point: "Sometimes the thoughts and actions of one character influence the thoughts and actions of another character; a sort of cross-character domino effect. Readers need to pay attention not only to how a single character's thoughts influence his or her own actions, but also the thoughts and actions of others in the story."

Teaching Point: "Often the problem in a story comes from two (or more) characters wanting different things that conflict. Readers need to consider the motivations of the main characters and how they do or don't go together."

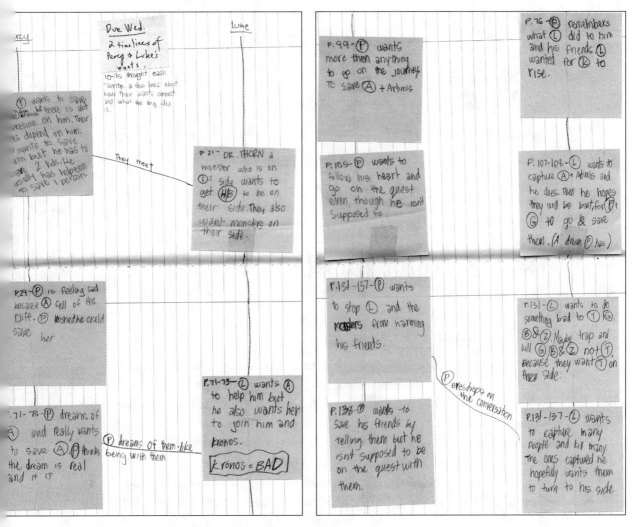

Figures 5.13a and 5.13b Fifth-grader Sky's timeline, tracking the "wants" (i.e., character motivations) of Percy and Luke from The Lightning Thief series.

PROJECT: Find *x* examples of places where two or more characters' thoughts and actions (and/or motivations) seem connected. Write a few sentences (or make a diagram, e.g., a timeline) showing how they are related (see Figures 5.13a and 5.13b).

⑥

Nuts and Bolts

Getting Started

Most students have been raised on a steady diet of pre-prepared comprehension questions, often drawn from reading programs and curriculum writers who have never met them. Hopefully more targeted are the questions coming from their classroom teachers, created with individual children in mind. In either case, the point is to assess students' understanding, and sometimes to nudge young readers to think about books in new ways. Both are important goals. Neither addresses the issue of kid independence.

After we leave school, no teacher sits on our shoulder telling us what to think about as we approach a complicated text. Certainly no one is there to help us figure out what to do when a passage is confusing. Being a reader involves making comprehension decisions on your own. To do this, we need a repertoire of strategies, and know when to call on which—depending on the text, and our purpose for reading.

The first step in introducing conference-based reading projects is to spend time teaching the larger purpose of becoming a skilled comprehension decision maker. Practically speaking, that means redefining what is expected in reading class and discussing the importance of being an independent reader. "That stuff is crucial, because without it they'll learn the structure of the conference but they're missing the most important part, which is that it's about their thinking," affirms Alycia Zimmerman, a third-grade teacher at PS 33. "They need to know that they are *already* thinking, and there is not just one way to do it. You need to understand that first, to know what to bring to the conference."

In addition to conveying the notion that there are many ways to think about your reading, there's also the expectation that an idea shouldn't stay the same from the beginning of the book to the end. The ability to adapt or revise your thinking does not come easily to most third through eighth graders. As Piaget reminds us, this is the concrete operational stage of development; once children get an idea, it's not so easy for them to change it. Young readers have difficulty letting their thinking evolve in reading for the same reason they struggle with revision in writing; once it's done, it's done. "You need to teach the idea of a line of thinking first," adds Joanne Searle, fifth-grade teacher at Manhattan New School. "Maybe what you think will be different after you've read for a bit, or maybe you'll think the same thing but have more evidence to back it up. Either way, your thoughts should grow."

For these reasons, it may be important to spend some time preparing a class before jumping into conference-based reading projects. Although there is no one right way to do it, what follows are some introductory lesson ideas from Alycia Zimmerman, with additional contributions from some other intrepid comprehension explorers. The recommendation is to do these lessons as early as possible in the school year, to set the stage for the idea that some of the students' work in reading will be these individual projects—and that there is an expectation that we will be doing independent thinking as we read. Teachers should feel free to do some, all, adapt, change, and hopefully modify the suggested language as befits the particular group of children in front of them.

Lesson One: What Do Readers Think About As They Read?

Rationale/Objective: Many students approach reading with a "What's the right answer?" mentality. In order for children to become flexible in their thinking, they need to have some sense of the different reasons people read—and know that, depending on their purpose for reading, two different people can think entirely different things about the *same* text. Often we are so busy telling students *what* to think about that we forget to check in and see which of these things have actually sunk in. This first lesson is really just a short conversation to take stock, followed by some independent reading.

Lesson/Sample Language:

1. *Preparation:* Prepare a sheet of blank chart paper or screen with the heading "What Do Readers Think About As They Read?"

2. Gather students in a meeting area, preferably where they normally come for read-alouds.

3. "Readers think about a lot of different things when they read. What are some of the things you think about when you read? Turn and talk."

4. Circulate among students for three or four minutes, taking notes of the ideas they are coming up with. It may be helpful to gently remind them of read-aloud discussions or other conversations about books that have happened in class.

5. Bring the class back together. Share some of what you've heard *in general terms, not related to a specific book*, listing their ideas on the chart or screen. (For example, if a student says, "We talked about how angry Katniss felt when her sister's name came up in the Reaping, and the way she jumped up and volunteered," we might write *The way characters feel and what their feelings make them do*.)

6. "Today, when you are reading your independent book, try to notice the kinds of things you start thinking about."

7. As students read, circulate and ask them what is happening in their book and what they are thinking about it. Take notes.

8. At the end of reading class, take a few minutes to report on what you've learned, adding your observations to the chart.

9. "It's interesting to see how many different *kinds* of things readers can think about. Whenever we read, it's important that we make choices about which of these things we want to stop and pay attention to."

Lesson Two: Ways We Think About Our Reading

Rationale/Objective: One of the biggest shifts for a class beginning conference-based reading projects is the notion that specific ideas we have about one book can sometimes apply to other books. When readers step back and think about the *types* of ideas they are having, they begin to develop a repertoire of different ways to think about texts.

Lesson Two uses talk as a springboard for looking at different lenses to think about texts. Ideally, this should be done over two days. The idea is to get students talking independently about a provocative, high-interest text; take a shorthand transcript of their conversation; examine the transcript with the class; and start what will become an ongoing list of "Ways We Think About

Our Reading." Looking at their own conversations, students not only begin to build a repertoire of entry points, but also recognize that kids in their class have particular reading personalities, i.e., things they are able to do as readers.

Truthfully, these sorts of independent conversations should not be thought of as just one lesson. After an initial introduction, they can become a class routine and occur once a week. A savvy teacher can leverage these conversations in individual or partner reading work (e.g., "You might want to try reading like Sophie today, and think about what seems unrealistic.") Best of all, this often results in students taking cues from one another independently—and trying out new ways of thinking about books without being told.

Lesson/Sample Language:

1. *Preparation:* Select a provocative, high-interest text to read aloud. This can be an article, short story, or poem. Another (recommended!) option is to use a chapter from an ongoing read aloud; that way the conversation and list can continue over several days.

2. "Yesterday we talked about some of the different ways a reader can think about a text. Today I am going to read you (*name the text*), and then we will get a chance to talk about it. My job will be to take notes on what you say." (*You may want to set up some ground rules to encourage students to listen and participate more actively. For example, have students call on one another to speak rather than the teacher doing it, or set up the expectation that the next speaker will begin by responding to the last one, etc.*)

3. Read the text aloud. Ham it up. Get kids excited.

4. An optional step might be to have students turn and talk to a partner or jot down their thoughts in a notebook before opening up the conversation to the whole class, to get ideas flowing.

5. Pick a student to begin the conversation. Don't be afraid to stack the deck in your favor; choose that reader you *know* will say something interesting. If the class has turned and talked, and/or jotted ahead of time, do a little spy work and find a ringer.

6. As students talk, take a transcript. (*Don't worry about getting down every word; you can tidy it up later.*) Resist the temptation to jump in and take over the conversation. A little wait time can go a long way.

7. After several students (as many as possible!) have spoken, stop the conversation and read back the transcript. "I'm going to read back what I got down. Speakers, please let me know whether I got it right; if I left something out or wrote it down wrong, tell me."

8. (*Next day, or another class period*) Project the transcript of the class conversation on a screen, or provide students with copies. Read through, stopping to name and note the *types of ideas* students had in the margins. Once again, name the ideas in general terms that can be applied to other books.

9. Start a list on chart paper of "Some of the Ways Our Class Thinks About What We Read" (see Figure 6.1).

10. "We've discussed how readers can think about texts in many different ways. Looking over this transcript, it's clear that in this class we have lots of different ways of looking at texts."

(*See the transcript and margin notes below, from Clarissa Isaac's third-grade class at PS 137, a high-poverty school on the Lower East Side of New York City. It's interesting to note how often the students refer back to something a classmate has said before; this is because the ground rule in the class was to build on earlier comments. Also note the teacher's shorthand, and the children's reflections on what went well/what to work on next, at the end of the transcript.*)

Third-grade conversation re: *Slower Than the Rest* by Cynthia Rylant

Prediction

Mariam: *I jotted that I predicted Leo would have the best project because he brought an object to show and tell.*

Main Idea

Lydia: *I agree with Mariam and want to add on—the main idea of the project was not what happens in the forest fire—the main idea was to show it's not fair to be slower than the rest—Leo compared himself to the turtle.*

Eve: *I agree with Lydia—think Leo and Charlie have a good connection—they were both slow—Charlie is slow and Leo learned differently—Leo relied on Charlie to feel better about himself and Charlie helped Leo with the project in school.*

Sophia: *I think Leo's father should not have told him "Slower than the rest"—what if father was slower when he was young?*

Zyaire: *I agree with Sophia—I want to make a connection to* Bridge to Terabithia*—Leo's dad same as Jess' dad—both put sons down in the beginning of the story.*

Text to Text Connection
Comparing Characters

Moments of silence—Recap the discussion (Teacher: "What idea can we talk more about?")

Janill: *I think the author compares Leo and Charlie by saying they are both slow—they are just not slow.*

Lydia: *Kind of agree—I think that being slow, not just physical, and he and Charlie are similar.*

Jessica: *I think Leo and Charlie have a connection—both slow in a different way. Also Charlie makes Leo feel like he is fast—not slow—Charlie gave him chance to win award—now he thinks he is fast.*

Compare and Contrast

Teona: *I think that—agree with Janill how Leo and Charlie are not slow in the same way—I want to add on when Leo won the award. I think he might go home, and his father might not think he is slow anymore.*

Ronasia: *I don't think boy was slow—he just learns in a slow type of way—he just learns differently—that's why they said he was slow.*

Inference, Author's Word Choice

Isaiah: *I agree with Lydia—being slow physical thing—Leo can't give up. He needs to keep practicing.*

Dominic: *I think like Lydia said, Leo is slow in some ways—turtle is also slow—I think he was trying to connect with turtle because it's not fair to be slow.*

Elicia: *I think if the father was in Leo's shoes—he wouldn't like it. Leo didn't like being called slow.*

Emiliano: *I agree with Elicia when she said that father should not call him really slow. Leo and Charlie are slow—Charlie is slow physically and Leo is slow mentally—he struggles with learning—not learning a lot and slowly.*

Walking in Character's Shoes

Mariam: If I was Leo I wouldn't give up my chance—keep on practicing.

Jasmine: I think that Leo felt sad when he was put in a slow class—he was not that smart—but he felt fast at the end.

Imani: I agree with Lydia and other people because it's like Charlie is slow and Leo is slow.

Jessica: I think I understand what Imani is trying to say—Leo is trying to catch on because he is slow—can't do as other kids—connection to the turtle.

Isaiah: Emiliano said Charlie and Leo are slow in different ways.

Cause & Effect

Character Change

Zyaire: I want to go back to what Jessica said—Charlie made Leo's world feel different. Charlie is the missing piece of Leo—when Charlie wasn't there—he wasn't happy— when he found Charlie—he had something beautiful.

Elicia: Everything changed.

Character Feelings

Ronasia: I agree with Zyaire—he was sad—everyone said he was slow—he had Charlie— he was happy.

Text to Text Connection

Jessica: I want to make connection to what Zyaire said—I want to include connection to the story, Missing Piece—Leo without the turtle is still slow but with the turtle—he can catch up with everyone.

Teona: He won—he's not slow anymore—his dad is going to stop saying he is slow.

What we did well

- put ourselves in characters' shoes
- took turns—a lot of people talked
- compared relationships in the book
- disagreed respectfully
- connected with real life.

What we need to work on

- saying the same thing as someone else
- fewer people passing
- doing more agreeing and disagreeing
- not agree
- listening.

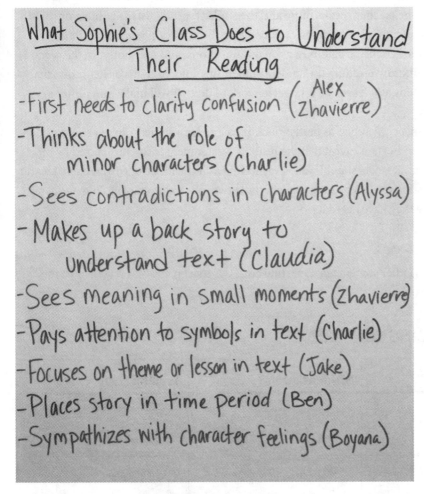

Figure 6.1 A chart naming the types of thinking students are doing in Sophie Brady's fifth-grade class at Manhattan New School

Lesson Three: Jobs in a Reading Conference

Rationale/Objective: It is difficult to do a good job at something when you don't know what your job *is*. When an activity involves two people, it is also helpful to know something about the role of the other participant. One of the reasons many students struggle with independent reading conferences is that no one has ever told them what they are supposed to do, let alone explained the job of the teacher.

In his seminal book *How's It Going?* writing conference guru Carl Anderson describes these two jobs clearly and succinctly. Put simply, a conference has two halves. In the first half of the conference, the student does most of the talking and the teacher mostly listens. In the second half, the roles switch; the teacher speaks more and the student mostly listens (Anderson 2000). In the first half, the student's job is to describe what he or she is working on and thinking about; the teacher's role is to listen carefully, ask a few questions, and take notes. In the second half, the teacher responds by teaching the student something tailored to his or her individual needs. The student listens and leaves with targeted work to do that will make him or her a better writer.

This "architecture of a conference" is pretty much the same for a student-driven reading conference—with the important caveat that the resulting assignment is co-constructed by the teacher *and* the student. Readers should walk away feeling as if the idea came from *them*. Lesson Three is pretty straightforward. We simply explain these two jobs to the student. In many cases, it will be the first time they have heard it.

Lesson/Sample Language:

1. *Preparation:* Gather students in a meeting area. On chart paper or a screen, post the following chart:

JOBS IN A READING CONFERENCE

	Student's Job	Teacher's Job
First half		
Second half		

2. "I'm pretty sure that every member of this class has had a reading conference in school before. A reading conference is when the teacher talks to you individually about the book you are reading. Thumbs up if you've had one."

3. "My guess is that even though you have had them before, you've probably never been told what your job is in a reading conference. You may never have even known that you *had* a job in a reading conference. And, if you ask me, it's hard to do a good job at something when you don't even know what your job *is*. So today, after all these years, I'm going to tell you what your job is in a reading conference—*and* I'm going to tell you what *my* job is. At the end, there will be a quiz. But don't worry, it's a quiz you will answer by pointing, and we'll all do it together."

4. (*During the following explanation, fill in the chart, as below.*) "It's pretty simple. A conference has two halves—a first half and a second half. In the first half, you have one job and in the second half, it switches. In the first half, *your* job is to do *most* of the talking. The teacher's job is to zip their lip and mostly listen."

JOBS IN A READING CONFERENCE

	Student's Job	Teacher's Job
First half	• Do most of the talking	• Mostly listen
Second half		

5. "Even though your job is to do most of the talking in the first half, you are not just supposed to be talking about what you like on your pizza. Your job is to tell *what you are thinking about your reading*. For example, you might think it's really unfair the way Peter always gets in trouble for what Fudge does, or you might think something that happens in your book is really unrealistic, or that a character should have acted in a different way. You see, I can find out what's happening in the book by reading it—but I can only know what *you* are thinking by talking to *you*. I may also ask you a few questions if I want to know more about something, and I will take notes. As your reading teacher, it's my job to study you as a reader. I need to know the sorts of things you think about and the things you are good at. Every person in this class is a little

different as a reader. So how can I be a good reading teacher for you if I don't know what *you* are especially good at?"

JOBS IN A READING CONFERENCE

	Student's Job	Teacher's Job
First half	• Do most of the talking • Tell what you are *thinking* about your book	• Mostly listen • Ask a few questions • Take notes
Second half		

6. "In the second half, the jobs switch. So who do you suppose does more listening in the second half? You can answer by pointing. Correct—it's you! And who does more of the talking? Right, it's the teacher. But my job isn't to just talk about whatever *I* want to talk about. The teacher helps you name something you want to think about, and together we come up with some work for you to do to explore your own idea."

JOBS IN A READING CONFERENCE

	Student's Job	Teacher's Job
First half	• Do most of the talking • Tell what you are *thinking* about your book	• Mostly listen • Ask a few questions • Take notes
Second half	• Do more listening • With teacher, come up with a special assignment to explore your idea	• Help student name something she or he wants to think about • With student, come up with an individual assignment to explore his or her idea

"So today I'll be having conferences with a few students. If you happen to be sitting near some-one who is having a conference, it's OK for you to listen in, as long as you don't interrupt. In fact, if you listen, then you will get to hear how a conference goes, so you can be ready when it's your turn. This type of work is going to help you practice coming up with your own ideas about what you read, so you don't have to always be told what to think about by a teacher."

Lesson Four: Watching How It's Done

Rationale/Objective: "Tell me, I'll forget. Show me, I'll remember. Involve me, I'll under-stand." This oft-quoted Chinese proverb is the rationale behind Lesson Four. Once they've heard an explanation of the jobs in a reading conference, it makes sense for children to observe one. Students watch as the teacher role-plays a student-driven reading conference with a colleague or student teacher. As they observe, children become "spies" and record what they notice.

To narrow the focus, Alycia Zimmerman recommends giving students a two-column obser-vation sheet. Half the class records what the "student" does, and the other half concentrates on the teacher's role. (See Figures 6.2a and 6.2b.)

Lesson/Sample Language:

1. *Preparation:*

    • Enlist a colleague, student teacher, or other adult to role-play a student-driven read-ing conference.

    • Choose a high-interest passage from a text familiar to students to discuss in the demonstration conference. (*A passage from a class read-aloud or whole-class book is ideal.*)

    • Call students to a meeting area with their pencils.

    • Give each student a two-column sheet labeled "Observations of What the Teacher Does in the Conference/Observations of What the Student Does in the Conference."

2. "Some of our reading work this year will be for everyone in the class to do. But we are also going to be doing independent work, where you get to come up with your own ideas and your own projects. That's what our reading conferences are for. We've already talked about what your job is and what the teacher's job is in a conference. Today, you are going to watch as Ms. _____ and I demonstrate. We are going to have a reading conference in front of you, and your challenge is to be a spy. Using this two-column sheet, half of the class is going to write down what they notice I

am doing as the teacher, and the other half of the class will be recording what Ms. _____ is doing as the student. By watching us, it will be easier to know what to do when it comes time for *your* reading conference."

3. Demonstrate a conference-based reading project, taking care that

   • the "teacher" asks the "student" to *say more* several times

   • the "student" refers to the text to provide evidence for her thinking

   • teacher and student negotiate an assignment together, including due date, format, number of examples, etc.

   • the teacher ends with a restatement of the teaching point, and how it will help the student beyond today's book.

4. Have students turn and talk, sharing their observations. Circulate and listen in, choosing students to share who will bring out the points listed above.

5. Bring the class together for a whole-class share, charting student's observations.

Lesson Five: Thinking Ahead About What to Say in Your Conference

Rationale/Objective: Almost anything goes more smoothly when it is rehearsed. Developmentally, children in the elementary and middle school years exist in the moment and are only just learning to think ahead. Lesson Five introduces the notion of anticipating what you might think about when you pick up your book; by planning ahead what to talk about, students are nudged to name their ongoing lines of thinking and are more prepared when it comes time for their conference. (See Figures 6.3a and 6.3b.)

Lesson/Sample Language:

1. *Preparation:* Cut up square sheets for each student to record what he or she plans to talk about during the reading conference. (*Samples from Alycia Zimmerman's class are shown in Figures 6.3a and 6.3b; choose your own wording!*)

2. "Now that we've begun our reading conferences and talked a lot about how they are supposed to go, it makes sense to begin thinking ahead of what you might want to talk about. Turn and tell your neighbor something you have been thinking about in your book that might be interesting to talk about in your conference."

3. Circulate as students discuss what they might talk about, listening for interesting ideas to share with the class.

My observations of what the "student" (Miss Rome) does in the conference	My observations of what the "student" (Miss Rome) does in the conference
• Wondering were charcter comes from • asks qustions (many) • Thinking about the meaning of the book. • Thinking about asking family or friends about book • favorite colors pink/purple	★ mrs Rome is focasing on her teacher. ★ she shows things that she does as a reader. ★ mrs rome has an assignments. ★ She has 2 days for her next confrence ★ She listens well to her teacher. ★ looked back at the text for clues and examples

My observations of what the teacher (Mrs. Zimmerman) does in the conference	My observations of what the teacher (Mrs. Zimmerman) does in the conference
She's asking questions. She's saying what type of things Jacky is good at. Using hand motions Reading story pointing at story Looking at Jacky as she talks. Give her post-its and assiment Asking how many days Jacky need Double checking if she knows her assiment	She asking a lot of qushtins. shes noticing things thats the stunden doing. shes asking the stundent to do a lot of things; shes helping her a lot. Shes asking the stundent to repent to see if shes lisning

Figures 6.2a and 6.2b Observations by Alycia Zimmerman's third graders of a conference-based reading project between Ms. Zimmerman and her student teacher—PS 33, New York City

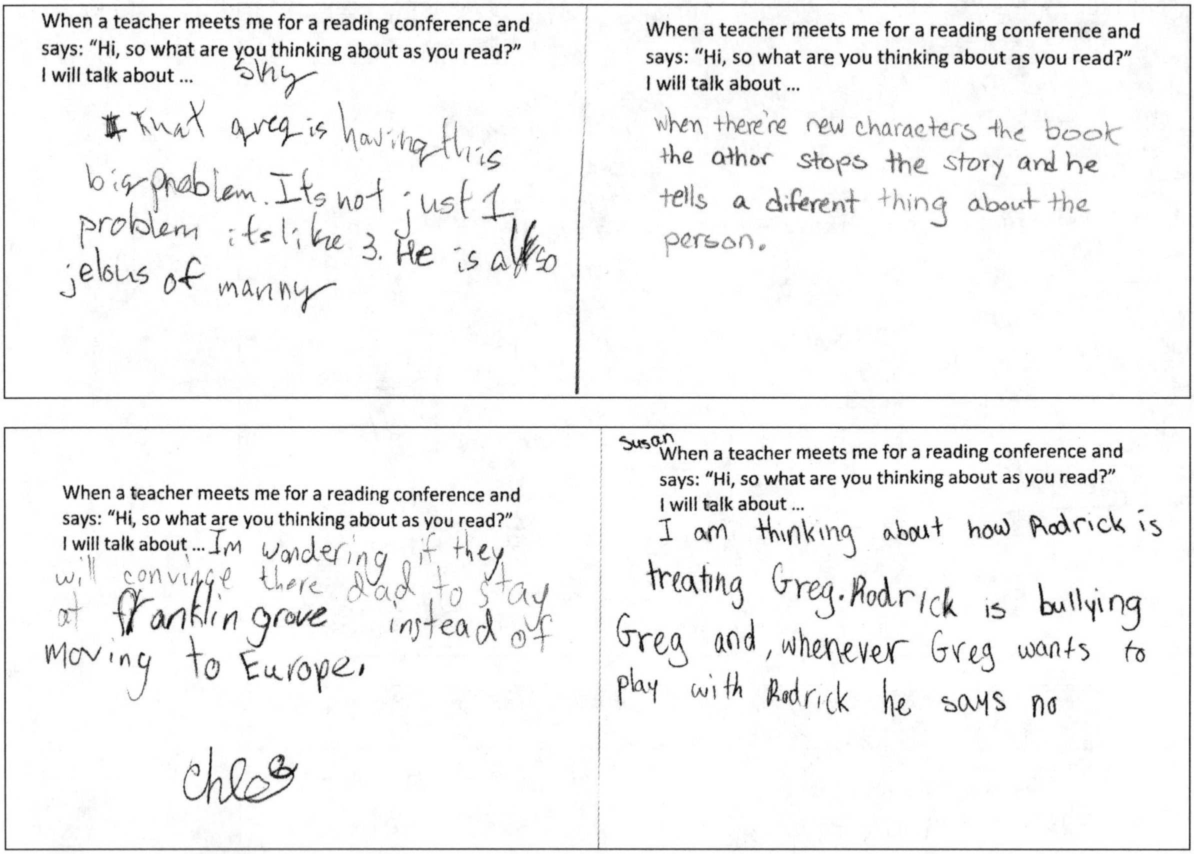

When a teacher meets me for a reading conference and says: "Hi, so what are you thinking about as you read?" I will talk about ... Sky

That greg is having this big problem. Its not just 1 problem its like 3. He is also jelous of manny

When a teacher meets me for a reading conference and says: "Hi, so what are you thinking about as you read?" I will talk about ...

when there're new characters the book the athor stops the story and he tells a diferent thing about the person.

When a teacher meets me for a reading conference and says: "Hi, so what are you thinking about as you read?" I will talk about ... Im wondering if they will convinge there dad to stay at franklin grove instead of moving to Europe.

chloe

Susan
When a teacher meets me for a reading conference and says: "Hi, so what are you thinking about as you read?" I will talk about ...

I am thinking about how Rodrick is treating Greg. Rodrick is bullying Greg and, whenever Greg wants to play with Rodrick he says no

Figures 6.3a and 6.3b What a few third graders from Alycia Zimmerman's class may talk about in their reading conferences

4. Bring the students back together. "Listening in to your conversations, I heard so many different ideas of things that could be interesting reading conference projects. For example, . . ." Name two or three different lines of thinking overheard during the turn and talk.

5. "When you get back to your seats, I will give each of you a small piece of paper to jot down a few words about what you might want to talk about at your conference." Show a sample square on a chart or document camera; perhaps demonstrate filling one in. "Thinking ahead about what you may want to talk about will help you get ready for the conference. It can also help get your mind ready for reading, since it will remind you of some of the ideas you have been having in this book."

Moving Forward, Allow Time for Sharing

Like most activities in the life of a classroom, conference-based reading projects succeed or fail in direct proportion to how big a deal we make of them. If they are treated as tangential to the regular reading curriculum and never discussed or celebrated publicly, chances are students will not take them seriously.

On the other hand, when a teacher allows time for children to share their individual reading projects with the rest of the class, they begin to feel a strong sense of ownership and involvement in their reading. "Since the class has been doing these projects," remarks Nancy Wahl, a fifth-grade teacher at PS 41, "they've become a community of readers in a way they never did before. There's a real sense that we are all coming up with our own, different ideas, and isn't that so interesting?"

Her students agree. "Sophia and I were reading partners," explained Dorentina, "and we were both reading *The City of Ember*. Ms. Wahl had conferences with each of us. My assignment was to pay attention to surprising parts in the book and think about what parts they connected to in earlier chapters. But Sophia was interested in looking at the clues. She put them in three groups—clues you think are important, but they aren't; ones that *don't* seem important, but it turns out they are; and clues that seem important, and you're right, they *are* important. So when we talked about the book together it was like we were getting ideas from each other—I hadn't ever thought about different kinds of clues, and she had never thought about paying attention to the surprising parts."

Many teachers find that setting aside a couple of times a week for students to share their reading projects has an exponential effect; kids not only start to get ideas from one another, but they sometimes want to try out a classmate's assignment with their own book.

"Sometimes I ask kids to share their project ideas right after the conference, before they've even done it, just to share the idea," says Nancy. "Other times, they'll present what they've come up with after they've finished. I try to get them all excited, telling them how cool it is that they are all doing their own work and that we can inspire each other in our reading. And it's not an act—it really *is* exciting. They come up with some amazing things!" (See Figure 6.4.)

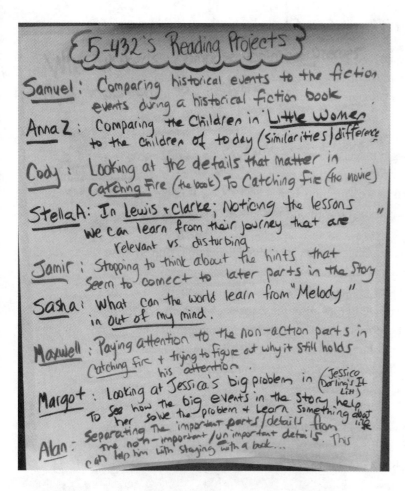

Figure 6.4 A chart from Nancy Wahl's fifth-grade classroom at PS 41. "Whenever a student shares a project, I add it to the chart. It's sort of a living document," Nancy explains. "The best part is when I see them looking at the chart on their own, and they start asking to try out each other's ideas."

Planning for Conferring, Conferring for Planning

It is impossible to plan out a good reading conference. The idea is to be in the moment and react to what the student says and does.

Wrong.

A good reading conference should be thoroughly planned. The teacher should go in with a preconceived notion of what to work on and a concrete expectation for the outcome.

Wrong again.

But at the same time, both are sort of true.

As an elementary principal, I frequently observed young teachers do demonstration lessons as part of our school's hiring process. It went without saying that they should show up well put together, with all their materials ready to go, and hand me a typed-up lesson plan. To not do so would be irresponsible, and I would likely not have taken them very seriously as candidates for the job. On the other hand, over time I began to notice that the applicants often fell into two categories. Some stuck to the lesson plan no matter what the kids said or did. Others were not afraid to take a detour when something unanticipated came up; though the lesson stayed on track, it did not end up looking exactly like what was typed on the paper. Most of the time I ended up hiring the latter type of teacher.

Business writer Kailash Awati writes in his blog *Eight to Late*:

> Planning is a result of conscious thought and deliberation whereas improvisation is a result of tacit knowledge being brought to bear, in an instant, on specific situations encountered in project (or other organizational) work. Nevertheless, despite their differences, both activities are important. . . . Efforts aimed at planning the future down to the last detail are misguided and bound to fail. *Contraria sunt complementa*: planning and improvisation are opposites, but they are complementary. (2011)

The truth is that though conference-based projects involve taking cues from students in the moment, a certain amount of forethought is required if they are to go well. Some planning considerations are more logistical, and have to do with getting around the classroom efficiently and keeping good records. Others are more concerned with thinking ahead to what we might want to address in a particular conference, based on what we know about the individual reader and his or her previous projects. Below are some things to keep in mind as a teacher prepares for project-based conferring.

Before and During

Decide in advance which students to confer with, consulting your notes in order to plan. Deciding then and there who to meet with on a given day can be a recipe for disaster. With the best of intentions, we are likely to see some students twice before conferring with others even once. It is best to go into a reading period already knowing which students you plan to meet with, taking into account where they sit in the room—we don't want to spend the entire class period in just one area.

It's also critical to look over your notes from previous conferences with these children ahead of time. Although it is important to be open to what comes up in today's conversation, it is also a good idea to connect to the last project; a good teaching point can often last for more than one conference, taking it a step further each time. Carl Anderson (2000) has famously urged teachers to begin writing conferences with the question "How's it going?" When you know a student well, this question does not have to be asked as though it is a blank slate. A teacher can ask how it's going *with* the strategy taught in the last conference. For example, you might ask, "How is it going stopping to think about surprising parts in *this* book?"

Think Ahead About How Long to Spend with Each Reader

Allow yourself a few short conferences (3–4 minutes), a couple of medium-length conferences (5–6 minutes), and one long one (7–8 minutes). Time yourself!

One of the biggest stumbling blocks for teachers getting started with conferring is time efficiency. With twenty-odd students in a class (at least!), how do you get to them all? Although there is no magic wand to make time stand still as we confer, one way to be more efficient is to plan ahead not just *who* to confer with but how long we will spend with each reader. Knowing that Ruby is pretty articulate and doing well with her synthesis work, you may want to allow just a four-minute, quick check-in conference to move things along. Adrian, on the other hand, is struggling a bit lately and it's unclear where to go next with him, so you'd better allow for a seven- or eight-minute conference.

Once you have decided on who and how long, it is a good idea to actually look at your watch and try your best to stick to these time limits. If things with Ruby go a little longer than expected, then shave a minute off of Adrian's conference. If a teacher doesn't adhere strictly to his or her own timetable, the conferring police are unlikely to make any arrests. "To be honest," says fourth-grade teacher Nikki Blaise of PS 15, "I hardly ever get it exact. But I definitely get more conferences done in this way than if I don't make a plan at all."

Take Notes During Each Conference

Record the

- key words/phrases used by the student
- assignment
- due date
- teaching point.

Whether you are the forgetful type or have a photographic memory, to remember the specific details of each student reading conference from day-to-day—let alone month-to-month, over the course of a school year—would be impossible. If these individual projects are to be an integral part of our reading instruction, it's important to develop a system for record keeping.

Some of the reasons for this are logistical. At the very least, a teacher needs to remember assignments and due dates. Since the first part of the conference relies heavily on asking students to *say more* about specific things, it's critical to get down exact words and phrases. Nothing signals careful listening better or makes children feel more important than when their teacher says their actual words back to them. This can be particularly powerful when students hear their own language repeated a week later, at the next conference. Sometimes a kid phrase can even supply the name for a strategy (see the Window Parts conference in Chapter 5).

In the bigger picture, a huge part of being successful with conference-based reading projects is connecting one conference to another. In order to do this, it is critical to have a record of each reader's teaching point. Ideally, we want to check in at the beginning of each conference on how it is going using the last strategy with the current text.

Some teachers like to design specific forms for their conferring notes, while others develop their own shorthand. Whatever the format, it is important to have a record of this specific information. Below are some examples of freehand conference notes from Eileen Delucia's seventh-grade class at PS/IS 7 in Spanish Harlem:

Linda B.—strong, good ideas, admits it when she doesn't understand—good at giving evidence—Book: *The Mediator*—about a girl who sees dead people—weird—(How?) She's not social—one dead girl, Heather, tries to kill Suzanna—"She's better with dead people than living" (a judgment—nice)—L gets gist and comes up with big ideas/judgments, but glosses over detail—find a part that shows difference in how she is with dead vs. living

Teaching Point: *readers notice how same character acts differently, has more than one side to them

Assignment: 3 ex each of how she is with dead/living, then write a few sentences about the diff, w/evidence

Lexis—a bit spacy, but makes good connections—needs help, not independent—Book: *Phoenix Rising*—tells how they are living with their sheep (he is conscious of the setting, also the book's main problem)—nuclear power plant explodes—radiation spreads—some reacting calmly—"Ripley is a problem, Nyla more reasonable"—(Who are you more like?) good with retell, very detailed, able to compare/contrast characters, with scaffolding—passive rdr., doesn't react emotionally

<u>T.P.:</u> *Readers react personally, yell, get annoyed, argue with the text

<u>A:</u> 5 ex of places where you want to yell at Ripley

After

Look across your conferring notes, making note of individual teaching points, strengths, needs, and end-year objectives. Where do lessons need to be elaborated on/reviewed/extended? Should they be done with individuals, small groups, or with the whole class?

"From an assessment point of view, the conference projects help me know what kids are actually thinking and doing, independently of what I think I've taught them," says upper elementary teacher Lauren Brown. "If you've just taught a lesson about symbolism and then say 'Go look for symbolism,' the work in your classroom is going to appear to be a lot stronger. You've just given them a formula, so if you assess right away, it's like 'Success! They understand symbolism! Good for me!' The real question is, six weeks down the road, how is that playing out in your room? Like how nice—I've created this little army of mini-Laurens who on this one day, for this one hour of time, can repeat back to me the brilliant thing I had to say about symbolism. In the conference-based projects, you see the difference between what you think you've taught them and what they actually know how to use on their own."

The truth is, as Lauren points out, most kids will do a serviceable job approximating a particular skill or strategy immediately after watching a teacher demonstrate. The question is, will they begin to incorporate this new knowledge into their independent thinking, when no one is specifically asking for it?

Though conference-based reading projects are targeted to the individual child and not just repetitions of whole-class curriculum, they are also valuable as assessment. Looking across conference notes, it becomes evident which strategies we have taught that students are beginning to use on their own—and which they are not. A teacher can then make decisions about how to follow up on what has not become part of a student's independent repertoire. If it's just a couple of kids, can it be addressed through partner work? Pockets of three or four students can be put together for small-group instruction—see Jennifer

Serravallo's *Teaching Reading in Small Groups* (2010) for ideas on how to do this effectively. Of course, if enough children do not understand how to apply a comprehension strategy to their independent reading, it may be time to revisit it in a whole-class lesson.

In the end, a good reading classroom introduces students to new ideas and strategies—but we are only doing half the job if young readers don't know when or how to use them on their own. Connecting end-year, whole-class objectives for reading with conference-based, individual reading projects is one way to help children become good comprehension decision makers.

And not for nothing; it makes them feel pretty jazzed about the work they are doing as readers working with their *own* ideas.

Works Cited

Allington, Richard. 2006. *What Really Matters for Struggling Readers.* 2nd ed. Boston, MA: Pearson.

Anderson, Carl. 2000. *How's It Going? A Practical Guide to Conferring with Student Writers.* Portsmouth, NH: Heinemann.

Awati, Kailash. 2012. "On the Ineffable Tacitness of Knowledge." *From Eight to Late* (blog). February 9, 2012. http://eight2late.wordpress.com/2012/02/09/on-the-ineffable-tacitness-of-knowledge/.

Babbitt, Natalie. 1975. *Tuck Everlasting.* New York: Farrar, Straus, and Giroux.

Brackett, Marc A. 2012. "The Ruler Approach to Social and Emotional Learning: Implications for Students, Teachers, and Leaders." PowerPoint presentation at the Health, Emotion, and Behavior Laboratory, Department of Psychology, Edward Zigler Center in Child Development and Social Policy, Yale University.

Brackett, Marc A., Susan E. Rivers, and Peter Salovey. 2011. "Emotional Intelligence: Implications for Personal, Social, Academic, and Workplace Success." *Social and Personality Psychology Compass* 5 (1): 88–103.

Calkins, Lucy. 1994. *The Art of Teaching Writing.* New ed. Portsmouth, NH: Heinemann.

Daniels, Harvey. Twitter Post, 2014. http://twitter.com/smokeylit.

Duke, Nell K., Samantha Caughlan, Mary Juzwik, and Nicole Martin. 2012. *Reading and Writing Genre with Purpose in K–8 Classrooms.* Portsmouth, NH: Heinemann.

Goodman, Yetta, and Gretchen Owocki. 2002. *Kidwatching: Documenting Children's Literacy Development.* Portsmouth, NH: Heinemann.

Holiday, Billie, and William Dufty. 1984. *Lady Sings the Blues: The Searing Autobiography of an American Musical Legend.* New York: Penguin.

Kasparov, Garry. 2007. *How Life Imitates Chess: Making the Right Moves, from the Board to the Boardroom.* New York: Bloomsbury USA.

Keene, Ellin. 2008. *To Understand: New Horizons in Reading Comprehension.* Portsmouth, NH: Heinemann.

———. 2012. *Talk About Understanding: Rethinking Classroom Talk to Enhance Comprehension*. Portsmouth, NH: Heinemann.

Keene, Ellin, and Susan Zimmermann. 1997. *Mosaic of Thought*. Portsmouth, NH: Heinemann.

———. 2007. *Mosaic of Thought*. 2nd ed. Portsmouth, NH: Heinemann.

Harvey, Stephanie, and Anne Goudvis. 2000. *Strategies That Work: Teaching Comprehension to Enhance Understanding*. Portland, ME: Stenhouse.

Jacques, Sophia, and Philip D. Zelazo. 2005. "Language and the Development of Cognitive Flexibility: Implications for Theory of Mind." In *Why Language Matters for Theory of Mind* 144–162, edited by Janet W. Astington and Jodie A. Baird. Oxford: Oxford University Press.

Johnston, Peter. 2004. *Choice Words: How Our Language Affects Children's Learning*. Portland, ME: Stenhouse.

———. 2012. *Opening Minds: Using Language to Change Lives*. Portland, ME: Stenhouse.

Lieberman, Matthew D., et al. 2007. "Putting Feelings Into Words: Affective Labeling Disrupts Amygdala Activity in Response to Affective Stimuli." *Psychological Science* 18 (5): 421–428.

Larsson, Stieg. 2005. *The Girl with the Dragon Tattoo*. New York: Vintage Books.

National Governors Association Center for Best Practices and Council of Chief State School Officers. 2010. *English Language Arts Standards*. Common Core State Standards Initiative. www.corestandards.org /ELA-literacy.

Nichols, Maria. 2006. *Comprehension Through Conversation: The Power of Purposeful Talk in the Reading Workshop*. Portsmouth, NH: Heinemann.

Serravallo, Jennifer. 2010. *Teaching Reading in Small Groups: Differentiated Instruction for Building Strategic, Independent Readers*. Portsmouth, NH: Heinemann.

Smith, Frank. 1983. "Reading Like a Writer." *Language Arts* 60 (5): 558–567.

Taylor, Barbara M., and P. David Pearson, eds. 2002. *Teaching Reading: Effective Schools, Accomplished Teachers*. Mahwah, NJ: Lawrence Erlbaum.

Tovani, Cris. 2011. *So What Do They Really Know? Assessment That Informs Teaching and Learning*. Portland, ME: Stenhouse.